Coffee Break Python

50 Workouts to Kickstart Your Rapid Code Understanding in Python

Christian Mayer

September 2018

A puzzle a day to learn, code, and play.

-) aktives Lernen viel effektiver als passives Lernen
-) "practice testing" besonders effektiv (testen, auch wenn man noch nicht alles weiß
-) ~~aktives lernen nicht verwechs~~ passives lernen alleine ist Zeitverschwendung;
-) Gewohnheiten sind mächtig; gute Gewohnheite können das ganze Leben verändern!
-) Es gibt keine Abkürzung! Lernen benötigt Zeit
-) Meister üben sich einen isolierten Stimulus, den sie immer wiederholen, bis sie ihn vollständig beherrschen
-) Schneller lerne in weniger Zeit es ruhig bleiben, sich die Zeit nehmen, tief einzusteigen.

-) Lernen durch Projekte: nur die halbe Wahrheit! ~~Theorie~~ verschiebt
die Grenze des Begrenzt durch tiefes Verständnis der Grundlagen. ->
Theorie + Praxis!
-) Warum stagnieren einige, andere werden Meister? -> Bücher
-) Sicherheit im Umgang mit Grundlagen
unterscheidet exzellente und durchschnittliche
Programmierer

Contents

— 1 —

Introduction

The great code masters—Knuth, Torvalds, and Gates—
share one character trait: the ambition to learn. If you
are reading this book, you are an aspiring coder and you
seek ways to advance your coding skills. You already have
some experience in writing code, but you feel that there
is a lot to be learned before you become a master coder.
You want to read and understand code better. You want
to challenge the status quo that some of your peers understand code faster than you. Or you are already proficient with another programming language like Java or
C++ but want to learn Python to become more valuable to the market place. Either way, you have already
proven your ambition to learn and, therefore, this book
is for you. To join the league of the great code masters,
you only have to do one thing: stay in the game.

The main driver for mastery is neither a character trait, nor talent. Mastery comes from intense, structured training. The author Malcolm Gladwell formulated the famous rule of 10,000 hours after collecting research from various fields such as psychology and neurological science.[1] The rule states that if you have average talent, you will reach mastery in any discipline by investing approximately 10,000 hours of intense training. Bill Gates, the founder of Microsoft, reached mastery at a young age as a result of coding for more than 10,000 hours. He was committed and passionate about coding and worked long nights to develop his skills. He was anything but an overnight success.

There is one thing that will empower *you* to invest the 10,000 hours of hard, focused work to reach mastery. What do you think it is? As for the code masters, it's *your ambition to learn* that will drive you through the valleys of desperation on your path to mastery: complex code, nasty bugs, and project managers pushing tight deadlines. Nurturing your ambition to learn will pay a rich stream of dividends to you and your family as long as you live. It will make you a respectable member of the society providing unique value to information technology, automation, and digitalization. Ultimately, it will give you strong confidence. So keeping your ambition to learn intact is the one thing you must place above all else.

---

[1]Malcolm Gladwell *Outliers: The Story of Success*

This book aims to be a stepping stone on your path to becoming a Python master. It helps you to learn faster by making use of the established principles of good teaching. It offers you ten to twenty hours of thorough Python training using one of the most efficient learning techniques, called *practice testing*. Investing this time will kickstart your skills to write, read, and understand Python source code.

The idea is that you solve code puzzles that start out simple but become more and more complex as you read the book. In essence, you play Python interpreter and compute the output of a code snippet in your head. Then you check whether you were right with your guess—using feedback and explanations—to adapt and improve your coding skills over time. To make this idea a reality, I developed the online coding academy `Finxter.com`. The next section explains and motivates the advantages of the Finxter method of puzzle-based learning.

— 2 —

A Case for Puzzle-based Learning

Definition: A *code puzzle* is an educative snippet of source code that teaches a single computer science concept by activating the learner's curiosity and involving them in the learning process.

Before diving into practical puzzle solving, let us first study 10 reasons why puzzle-based learning accelerates your learning speed and improves retention of the learned material. There is robust evidence in psychological science for each of these reasons. Yet, none of the existing coding books lift code puzzles to being first-class citizens. Instead, they are mostly focused on one-directional teaching. This book attempts to change that. In brief, the 10 reasons for puzzle-based learning are the following.

4

1. Overcome the Knowledge Gap (Section 2.1)

2. Embrace the Eureka Moment (Section 2.2)

3. Divide and Conquer (Section 2.3)

4. Improve From Immediate Feedback (Section 2.4)

5. Measure Your Skills (Section 2.5)

6. Individualized Learning (Section 2.6)

7. Small is Beautiful (Section 2.7)

8. Active Beats Passive Learning (Section 2.8)

9. Make Source Code a First-class Citizen (Section 2.9)

10. What You See is All There is (Section 2.10)

2.1 Overcome the Knowledge Gap

The great teacher Socrates delivered complex knowledge by asking a sequence of questions. Each question built on answers to previous questions provided by the student. This more than 2400 year old teaching technique is still in widespread use today. A good teacher opens a gap between their knowledge and the learner's. The knowledge gap makes the learner realize that they do not know the answer to a burning question. This creates a tension in the learner's mind. To close this gap, the learner awaits the missing piece of knowledge from the teacher. Better yet, the learner starts developing their own answers. The learner *craves knowledge*.

Code puzzles open an immediate knowledge gap. When looking at the code, you first do not understand the meaning of the puzzle. The puzzle's semantics are hidden. But only you can transform the unsolved puzzle into a solved one. Look at this riddle: "What pulls you down and never lets go?" Can you feel the tension? Opening and closing a knowledge gap is a very powerful method for effective learning.[1]

Bad teachers open a knowledge gap that is too large. The learner feels frustrated because they cannot overcome the gap. Suppose you are standing before a river that you must cross. But you have not learned to swim, yet. Now, consider two rivers. The first is the Colorado River that carved out the Grand Canyon—quite a gap. The second is Rattlesnake Creek. The fact that you have never heard of this river indicates that it is not too big of an obstacle. Most likely, you will not even attempt to swim through the big Colorado River. But you could swim over the Rattlesnake if you stretch your abilities just a little bit. You will focus, pep-talk yourself, and

---

[1] The answer is *Gravity*.

overcome the obstacle. As a result, your swimming skills and your confidence will grow a little bit.

Puzzles are like the Rattlesnake—they are not too great a challenge. You must stretch yourself to solve them, but you can do it, if you go all-out.

Constantly feeling a small but non-trivial knowledge gap creates a healthy learning environment. Stretch your limits, overcome the knowledge gap, and become better—one puzzle at a time.

2.2 Embrace the Eureka Moment

Humans are unique because of their ability to learn. Fast and thorough learning has always increased our chances of survival. Thus, evolution created a brilliant biological reaction to reinforce learning in your body. Your brain is wired to seek new information; it is wired to always process data, to always learn.

Did you ever feel the sudden burst of happiness after experiencing a eureka moment? Your brain releases endorphins, the moment you close a knowledge gap. The instant gratification from learning is highly addictive, but this addiction makes you smarter. Solving a puzzle gives your brain instant gratification. Easy puzzles open small, hard puzzles, which open large knowledge gaps. Overcome any of them and learn in the process.

2.3   Divide and Conquer

Learning to code is a complex task. You must learn a myriad of new concepts and language features. Many aspiring coders are overwhelmed by the complexity. They seek a clear path to mastery.

People tend to prioritize specific activities with clearly defined goals. If the path is not clear, we tend to drift away toward more specific paths. Most aspiring coders think they have a goal: becoming a better coder. Yet, this is not a specific goal at all. So what is a specific goal? *Watching Game of Thrones after dinner, Series 2 Episode 1* is as specific as it can be. Due to the specificity, watching Netflix is more powerful than the fuzzy path of learning to code. Hence, watching Netflix wins most of the time.

As any productivity expert will tell you: break a big task or goal into a series of smaller steps. Finishing each tiny step brings you one step closer to your big goal. *Divide and conquer* makes you feel in control, pushing you one step closer toward mastery. You want to become a master coder? Break the big coding skill into a list of sub-skills—understanding language features, designing algorithms, reading code—and then tackle each sub-skill one at a time.

Code puzzles do this for you. They break up the huge task of learning to code into a series of smaller learning units. The student experiences laser focus on one learning task such as *recursion*, the *for loop*, or *keyword arguments*. Don't worry if you do not understand these concepts yet—after working through this book, you will. A good code puzzle delivers a single idea from the author's into the student's head. You can digest one puzzle at a time. Each puzzle is a step toward your bigger goal of mastering computer science. Keep solving puzzles and you keep improving your skills.

2.4   Improve From Immediate Feedback

As a child, you learned to walk by trial and error—try, receive feedback, adapt, and repeat. Unconsciously, you will minimize negative and maximize positive feedback. You avoid falling because it hurts, and you seek the approval of your parents. But not only organic life benefits from the great learning technique of trial and error. In machine learning, algorithms learn by guessing an output and adapting their guesses based on their correctness. To learn anything, you need feedback such that you can adapt your actions.

However, an excellent learning environment provides you not only with feedback but with *immediate* feedback for your actions. In contrast, poor learning environments do not provide any feedback at all or only with a large delay. Examples are activities with good short-term and bad long-term effects such as smoking, alcohol, or damaging the environment. People cannot control these activities because of the delayed feedback. If you were to slap your friend each time he lights a cigarette—a not overly drastic measure to safe his life—he would quickly stop smoking. If you want to learn fast, make sure that your environment provides immediate feedback. Your brain will find rules and patterns to maximize the reinforcement from the immediate feedback.

This book offers you an environment with immediate feedback to make learning to code easy and fast. Over time, your brain will absorb the meaning of a code snippet quicker and with higher precision this way. Learning this skill pushes you toward the top 10% of all coders. There are other environments with immediate feedback, like executing code and checking correctness, but puzzle-based learning is the most direct one: Each puzzle educates with immediate feedback.

2.5   Measure Your Skills

You need to have a definite goal to be successful. A definite goal is a powerful motivator and pushes you to stretch your skills constantly. The more definite and concrete it is, the stronger it becomes. Holding a definite goal in your mind is the first and foremost step toward its physical manifestation. Your beliefs bring your goal into reality.

Think about an experienced Python programmer you know, e.g., your nerdy colleague or class mate. How good are their Python skills compared to yours? On a scale from your grandmother to Bill Gates, where is your colleague and where are you? These questions are difficult to answer because there is no simple way to measure the skill level of a programmer. This creates a severe problem for your learning progress: the concept of being a good programmer becomes fuzzy and diluted. What you can't measure, you can't improve. Not being able to measure your coding skills diverts your focus from systematic improvement. Your goal becomes less definite.

So what should be your definite goal when learning a programming language? To answer this, let us travel briefly to the world of chess, which happens to provide an excellent learning environment for aspiring players. Every player has an Elo rating number that measures their skill level. You get an Elo rating when playing against other players—if you win, your Elo rating increases. Victories against stronger players lead to a higher increase of the Elo rating. Every ambitious chess player simply focuses on one thing: increasing their Elo rating. The ones that manage to push their Elo rating very high, earn grand master titles. They become respected among chess players and in the outside world.

Every chess player dreams of being a grandmaster. The goal is as definite as it can be: reaching an Elo of 2400 and master level (see Section 3). Thus, chess is a great learning environment—every player is always aware of their skill level. A player can measure how decisions and habits impact their Elo number. Do they improve when sleeping enough before important games? When training opening variants? When solving chess puzzles? What you can measure, you can improve.

The main idea of this book, and the associated learning app `Finxter.com,` is to transfer this method of measuring skills from the chess world to programming. Suppose you want to learn Python. The Finxter website assigns you a rating number that measures your coding skills. Every Python puzzle has a rating number as well, according to its difficulty level. You 'play' against a puzzle at your difficulty level: The puzzle and you will have more or less the same Elo rating so that you can enjoy personalized learning. If you solve the puzzle, your Elo increases and the puzzle's Elo decreases. Otherwise, your Elo decreases and the puzzle's Elo increases. Hence, the Elo ratings of the difficult puzzles increase over time. But only learners with high Elo ratings will see them. This self-organizing system ensures that you are always challenged but not overwhelmed, while you constantly receive feedback about how good your skills are in comparison with others. You always know exactly where you stand on your path to mastery.

2.6 Individualized Learning

The educational system today is built around the idea of classes and courses. In these environments, all students consume the same learning material from the same teacher applying the same teaching methods. This traditional idea of classes and courses has a strong foundation in our culture and social thinking patterns. Yet, science proves again and again the value of individualized learning. Individualized learning tailors the content, pace, style, and technology of teaching to the student's skills and interests. Of course, truly individualized learning has always required a lot of teachers. But paying a high number of teachers is expensive (at least in the short term) in a non-digital environment.

In the digital era, many fundamental limitations of our society begin to crack. Compute servers and intelligent machines can provide individualized learning with ease. But with changing limitations, we must adapt our thinking as well. Machines will enable truly individualized learning very soon; yet society needs time to adapt to this trend.

Puzzle-based learning is a perfect example of auto-

mated, individualized learning. The ideal puzzle stretches
the student's abilities and is neither boring nor overwhelming. Finding the perfect learning material for each
learner is an important and challenging problem. Finxter uses a simple but effective solution to solve this problem: the Elo rating system. The student solves puzzles
at their individual skill level. This book and the book's
web backend Finxter pushes teaching toward individualized learning.

2.7 Small is Beautiful

The 21st century has seen a rise in microcontent. Microcontent is a short and accessible piece of valuable information such as the weather forecast, a news headline,
or a cat video. Social media giants like Facebook and
Twitter offer a stream of never-ending microcontent. Microcontent is powerful because it satisfies the desire for
shallow entertainment. Microcontent has many benefits:
the consumer stays engaged and interested, and it is easily digestible in a short time. Each piece of microcontent
pushes your knowledge horizon a bit further. Today, millions of people are addicted to microcontent.

However, this addiction will also become a problem to
these millions. The computer science professor Cal New-
port shows in his book *Deep Work* that modern society
values deep work more than shallow work. Deep work is

a high-value activity that needs intense focus and skill. Examples of deep work are programming, writing, or researching. Contrarily, shallow work is every low-value activity that can be done by everybody (e.g., posting the cat videos to social media). The demand for deep work grew with the rise of the information society; at the same time, the supply stayed constant or decreased, e.g., because of the addictiveness of shallow social media. People that see and understand this trend can benefit tremendously. In a free market, the prices of scarce and demanded resources rise. Because of this, surgeons, lawyers, and software developers earn $100,000 per year and more. Their work cannot easily be replaced or outsourced to unskilled workers. If you are able to do deep work, to focus your attention on a challenging problem, society pays you generously.

What if we could marry the concepts of microcontent and deep work? This is the promise of puzzle-based learning. Finxter offers a stream of self-contained microcontent in the form of hundreds of small code puzzles. But instead of just being unrelated microcontent, each puzzle is a tiny stimulus that teaches a coding concept or language feature. Hence, each puzzle pushes your knowledge *in the same direction.*

Puzzle-based learning breaks the bold goal, i.e., *reach the mastery level in Python*, into tiny actionable steps: solve and understand one code puzzle per day. While solving the smaller tasks, you progress toward your larger goal. You take one step at a time to eventually reach the mastery level. A clear path to success.

2.8 Active Beats Passive Learning

Robust scientific evidence shows that active learning doubles students' learning performance. In a study on that matter, test scores of active learners improve by more than one grade compared to their passive learning fellow students.[2] Not using active learning techniques wastes your time and hinders you in reaching your full potential in any area of life. Switching to active learning is a simple tweak that will instantly improve your performance when learning any subject.

How does active learning work? Active learning requires the student to interact with the material, rather than simply consuming it. It is student- rather than teacher-centric. Great active learning techniques are asking and answering questions, self-testing, teaching, and summarizing. A popular study shows that one of the best learning techniques is *practice testing*.[3] In this learning technique, you test your knowledge even if you have not

---

[2]   https://en.wikipedia.org/wiki/Active_learning#Research_evidence

[3]   http://journals.sagepub.com/doi/abs/10.1177/1529100612453266

learned everything yet. Rather than *learning by doing,* it's *learning by testing.*

However, the study argues that students must feel safe during these tests. Therefore, the tests must be low-stake, i.e., students have little to lose. After the test, students get feedback about the correctness of the tests. The study shows that practice testing boosts long-term retention of the material by almost a factor of 10. As it turns out, solving a daily code puzzle is not just another learning technique—it is one of the best.

Although active learning is twice as effective, most books focus on passive learning. The author delivers information; the student passively consumes the information. Some programming books include active learning elements by adding tests or by asking the reader to try out the code examples. Yet, I always found this impracticable while reading on the train, on the bus, or in bed. But if these active elements drop out, learning becomes 100% passive again.

Fixing this mismatch between research and common practice drove me to write this book about puzzle-based learning. In contrast to other books, this book makes active learning a first-class citizen. Solving code puzzles is an inherent active learning technique. You must develop the solution yourself, in every single puzzle. The teacher is as much in the background as possible—they

only explain the correct solution if you couldn't work it
out yourself. But before telling you the correct solution,
your knowledge gap is already ripped wide open. Thus,
you are mentally ready to digest new material.

To drive this point home, let me emphasize this argument again: puzzle-based learning is a variant of the
active learning technique named practice testing. Practice testing is scientifically proven to teach you more in
less time.

2.9 Make Code a First-class Citizen

Each grandmaster of chess has spent tens of thousands
of hours looking into a near infinite number of chess positions. Over time, they develop a powerful skill: the intuition of the expert. When presented with a new position,
they are able to name a small number of strong candidate
moves within seconds. They operate on a higher level
than normal people. For normal people, the position of
a single chess piece is one chunk of information. Hence
they can only memorize the position of about six chess
pieces. But chess grand masters view a whole position or
a sequence of moves as a single chunk of information. The
extensive training and experience has burned strong patterns into their biological neural networks. Their brain

is able to hold much more information—a result of the good learning environment they have put themselves in.

What are some principles of good learning? Let us dive into another example of a great learning environment—this time for machines. Recently, Google's artificial intelligence AlphaZero has proven to be the best chess playing entity in the world. AlphaZero uses artificial neural networks. An artificial neural network is the digital twin of the human brain with artificial neurons and synapses. It learns by example much like a grandmaster of chess. It presents itself a position, predicts a move, and adapts its prediction to the extent the prediction was incorrect.

Chess and machine learning exemplify principles of good learning that are valid in any field you want to master. First, transform the object to learn into a stimulus that you present to yourself over and over again. In chess, study as many chess positions as you can. In math, make reading mathematical papers with theorems and proofs a habit. In coding, expose yourself to lots of code. Second, seek feedback. Immediate feedback is better than delayed feedback. However, delayed feedback is still much better than no feedback at all. Third, take your time to learn and understand thoroughly. Although it is possible to learn on-the-go, you will cut corners. The person who prepares beforehand always has an edge. In the world of coding, some people recommend learning by coding practical projects and doing nothing more. Chess

↳ vgl Kindle - Buch : neue Sprache lernen

grandmasters, sports stars, and intelligent machines do not follow this advice. They learn by practicing isolated stimuli again and again until they have mastered them. Then they move on to more complex stimuli.

Puzzle-based learning is code-centric. You will find yourself staring at the code for a long time until the insight strikes. This creates new synapses in your brain that help you understand, write, and read code fast. Placing code in the center of the whole learning process creates an environment in which you will develop the powerful intuition of the expert. *Maximize the learning time you spend looking at code rather than at other stimuli.*

2.10 What You See is All There is

My professor of theoretical computer science used to tell us that if we only stare long enough at a proof, the meaning will transfer into our brains by osmosis. This fosters deep thinking, a state of mind where learning is more productive. In my experience, his staring method works—but only if the proof contains everything you need to know to solve it. It must be self-contained.

A good code puzzle beyond the most basic level is self-contained. You can solve it purely by staring at it until your mind follows your eyes—your mind develops a solution based on rational thinking. There is no need to look things up. If you are a great programmer, you will find the solution quickly. If not, it will take more time but you can still find the solution—it is just more challenging.

My gold standard was to design each puzzle such that it is mostly self-contained. However, to deliver on the book's promise of training your understanding of the Python basics, puzzles must introduce syntactical language elements as well. But even if the syntax in a puzzle challenges you, you should still develop your own solutions based on your imperfect knowledge. This probabilistic thinking opens the knowledge gap and prepares your brain to receive and digest the explained solution. After all, your goal is long-term retention of the material.

— 3 —

The Elo Rating for Python

Pick any sport you always loved to do. How good are you compared to others? The Elo rating answers this question with surprising accuracy. It assigns a number to each player that represents their skill in the sport. The higher the Elo number, the better the player.

Let us give a small example of how the Elo rating works in chess. Alice is a strong player with an Elo rating of 2000 while Bob is an intermediate player with Elo 1500. Say Alice and Bob play a chess game against each other. Who will win the game? As Alice is the stronger player, she should win the game. The Elo rating system rewards players for good and punishes for bad results: the better the result, the higher the reward. For Bob, a win, or even a draw, would be a very good outcome of the game. For Alice, the only satisfying result is a win. Winning against a weaker player is less rewarding than winning against a stronger player. Thus, the Elo rating system rewards Alice with only +3 Elo points for a win. A loss costs her -37 Elo points, and even a draw costs her -17 points. Playing against a weaker player is risky for her because she has much to lose but little to win.

The idea of Finxter is to view your learning as a series of games between two players: you and the Python puzzle. Both players have an Elo rating. Your rating measures your current skills and the puzzle's rating reflects the difficulty. On our website `finxter.com`, a puzzle plays against hundreds of Finxter users. Over time, the puzzle's Elo rating converges to its true difficulty level.

Table 3.1 shows the ranks for each Elo rating level. The table is an opportunity for you to estimate your Python skill level. In the following, I describe how you can use this book to test your Python skills.

3.1 How to Use This Book

This book provides a series of 50 code puzzles plus explanations to test and train your Python skills. The puzzles start from beginner level and become gradually harder to reach intermediate level. A follow-up book covers intermediate to expert level. This book is perfect for users between the beginner and the intermediate level. Yet,

Elo rating	Rank
2500	World Class
2400-2500	Grandmaster
2300-2400	International Master
2200-2300	Master
2100-2200	National Master
2000-2100	Master Candidate
1900-2000	Authority
1800-1900	Professional
1700-1800	Expert
1600-1700	Experienced Intermediate
1500-1600	Intermediate
1400-1500	Experienced Learner
1300-1400	Learner
1200-1300	Scholar
1100-1200	Autodidact
1000-1100	Beginner
0-1000	Basic Knowledge

Table 3.1: Elo ratings and skill levels.

even expert users can improve their speed of code understanding. No matter your current skill level, you will benefit from puzzle-based learning. It will deepen and accelerate your understanding of basic coding patterns.

3.2   The Ideal Code Puzzle

The ideal code puzzle possesses each of the following six properties. The puzzle

1. has a surprising result;

2. provides new information;

3. is relevant and practical;

4. delivers one main idea;

5. can be solved by thinking alone; and

6. is challenging but not overwhelming.

This was the gold standard for all the puzzles created in this book. I did my best to adhere to this standard.

3.3 How to Exploit the Power of Habits?

You are what you repeatedly do. Your habits determine your success in life and in any specific area such as coding. Creating a powerful learning habit can take you a long way on your journey to becoming a code master. Charles Duhigg, a leading expert in the psychology of habits, shows that each habit follows a simple process called the *habit loop*. This process consists of three steps: trigger, routine, and reward.[1] First, the trigger starts the process. A trigger can be anything such as drinking your morning coffee. Second, the routine is an action you take when presented with the trigger. An example routine is to solve a code puzzle. Each routine is in anticipation of a reward. Third, the reward is anything that makes you feel good. When you overcome a knowledge gap, your brain releases endorphins—a powerful reward. Over time, your habit becomes stronger—you seek the reward.

Habits with strong manifestations in these three steps are life-changing. Invest 10% of your paycheck every month and you will be rich one day. Get used to the habit of solving one Python puzzle a day as you drink your morning coffee—and enjoy the endorphin dose in your brain. Implementing this *Finxter loop* in your day

---

[1] Charles Duhigg, *The Power of Habit: Why We Do What We Do in Life and Business.*

sets up an automatic progress toward you becoming a better and better coder. As soon as you have established the Finxter loop as a strong habit, it will cost you neither a lot of time, nor energy. This is self-engineering at its finest level.

3.4 How to Test and Train Your Skills?

I recommend solving at least one or two code puzzles every day, e.g., as you drink your morning coffee. Then you spend the rest of your learning time on real projects that matter to you. The puzzles guarantee that your skills improve over time and the real project brings you results.

If you want to test your Python skills, use the following simple method.

1. Track your individual Elo rating as you read the book and solve the code puzzles. Simply write your current Elo rating into the book. Start with an initial rating of 1000 if you are a beginner, 1500 if you are an intermediate, and 2000 if you are an advanced Python programmer. Of course, if you already have an online rating on `finxter.com`, starting with this rating would be the most precise op-

tion. Figure 3.4 shows five different examples of how your Elo will change while working through the book. Two factors impact the final rating: how you select your initial rating and how good you perform (the latter being more important).

2. If your solution is correct, add the Elo points according to the table given with the puzzle. Otherwise, subtract the given Elo points from your current Elo number.

Solve the puzzles in a sequential manner because they build upon each other. Advanced readers can also solve puzzles in the sequence they wish—the Elo rating will work as well. The Elo rating will become more accurate as you solve more and more puzzles. Although only an estimate, your Elo rating is an objective measure to compare your skills with the skills of others. Several Finxter users have reported that the rating is surprisingly accurate.

Use the following training plan to develop a strong learning habit with puzzle-based learning.

1. Select a daily trigger after which you solve code puzzles for 10 minutes. For example, decide on your *Coffee Break Python*, or even solve code puzzles as you brush your teeth or sit on the train to work, university, or school.

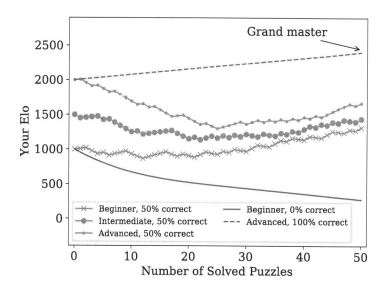

Figure 3.1: This plot exemplifies how your Elo rating may change while you work through the 50 code puzzles. There are three important observations. First, no matter how you select your initial Elo, you will converge to your true skill level as you solve more puzzles. Second, you will lose Elo points faster when you have a higher Elo number. Third, your final Elo will be anywhere between 200 and 2450 after working through this book.

2. Scan over the puzzle in a first quick pass and ask yourself: what is the unique idea of this puzzle?

3. Dive deeply into the code. Try to understand the purpose of each symbol, even if it seems trivial at first. Avoid being shallow and lazy. Instead, solve each puzzle thoroughly and take your time. It's counterintuitive: To learn faster in less time, you must stay calm and take your time and allow yourself to dig deep. There is no shortcut.

4. Make sure you carry a pen with you and write your solution into the book. This ensures that you stay objective—we all have the tendency to fake ourselves. Active learning is a central idea of this book.

5. Look up the solution and read the explanation with care. Do you understand every aspect of the code? Write open questions down and look them up later, or send them to me (`info@finxter.com`). I will do everything I can to come up with a good explanation.

6. Only if your solution was 100% correct—including whitespaces, data types, and formatting of the output—you get Elo points for this puzzle. Otherwise you should count it as a wrong solution and swallow the negative Elo points. The reason for this strict rule

is that this is the best way to train yourself to solve the puzzles thoroughly.

As you follow this simple training plan, your skill to see through source code quickly will improve. Over the long haul, this will have a huge impact on your career, income, and work satisfaction. You do not have to invest much time because the training plan requires only 10–20 minutes per day. But you must be persistent in your training effort. If you get off track, get right back on track the next day. When you run out of code puzzles, feel free to checkout `Finxter.com` with more than 300 hand-crafted code puzzles. I regularly publish new code puzzles on the website as well.

3.5 What Can This Book Do For You?

Before we dive into puzzle solving, let me anticipate and address possible misconceptions about this book.

The puzzles are too easy/too hard. This book is for you if you already have some experience in coding. Your skill level in the Python programming language ranges from beginner to intermediate. Even so, if you are already an advanced coder, this book is for you as well—if you read it in a different way. Measure the time you need to solve the puzzles and limit your solution time to only 10–20 seconds. This introduces an additional challenge for solving the puzzles: time pressure. Solving puzzles under time pressure sharpens your rapid code understanding skills even more. Eventually, you will feel that your coding intuition has improved. If the puzzles are too hard, great. Your knowledge gap must be open before you can effectively absorb information. Just take your time to thoroughly understand every bit of new information. Study the cheat sheets in Chapter 4 properly.

This book is not conventionally structured by topic. Correct, the puzzles are sorted by Elo and not structured by topic. Puzzles with a small Elo rating are easier and more fundamental. Puzzles with a higher Elo rating are harder. To solve them, you need to combine the fundamental learnings from the easier puzzles. Ordering puzzles by difficulty has many advantages. You can solve puzzles in your skill level. As you are getting better, the puzzles become harder. Finally, ordering by complexity allows us to combine many topics in a single puzzle. For example, a Python one-liner may use two topics: list comprehension and lambda functions.

Learning to code is best done via coding on projects. This is only part of the truth. Yes, you can improve your skills to a certain level by diving into practical projects. But as in every other discipline, your skills will bounce quickly against your personal ceiling. Your ceiling is the maximum skill level you are able to reach, given your current limitations. These limitations come from a lack of thorough understanding of basic knowledge. You cannot understand higher-level knowledge properly without understanding the basic building blocks. Have you ever used machine learning techniques in your work? Without theoretical foundations, you are doomed. Theory pushes your ceiling upwards and gets rid of the limitations that hold you back.

Abraham Lincoln said: *"Give me six hours to chop down a tree and I will spend the first four sharpening the axe."* Do not fool yourself into the belief that *just doing it* is the most effective road to reach any goal. You must constantly sharpen the saw to be successful in any discipline. Learning to code is best done via practical coding *and* investing time into your personal growth. Millions of computer scientists enjoyed an academic education. They know that solving hundreds or thousands of toy examples in their studies built a strong and thorough foundation.

How am I supposed to solve this puzzle if I do not know the meaning of this specific Python language feature? Guess it! Python is an intuitive language. Think about potential meanings. Solve the puzzle for each of them—a good exercise for your brain. The more you work on the puzzle, even with imperfect knowledge, the better you prepare your brain to absorb the puzzle's explanation.

Why should I buy the book when puzzles are available for free at Finxter. com? My goal is to remove barriers to learning Python. Thus, all puzzles are available for free online. This book is based on the puzzles available at Finxter, but it extends them with more detailed and structured information. Nevertheless, if you don't like reading books, feel free to check out the website.

Anyway, why do some people thrive in their fields and become valued experts while others stagnate? They read books in their field. They increase their value to the marketplace by feeding themselves with valuable information. Over time, they have a huge advantage over their peers. They get the opportunities to develop themselves even further. They enjoy their jobs and have much higher work satisfaction and life quality. Belonging to the top ten percent in your field yields hundreds of thousands of dollars during your career. However, there is price you have to pay to unlock the gates to this world: you have to invest in books and your own personal development. The more time and money you spend on books, the more valuable you become to the marketplace!

The Elo-based rating is not accurate. Several finxters find the rating helpful, fair, and accurate in comparison to others. It provides a good indication of where one stands in the field of Python coders. If you feel the rating is not accurate, ask yourself whether you are objective. If you think you are, please let me know so that I have a chance to improve this book and the Finxter back-end.

−)

A Quick Overview of the Python Language

Before diving into the puzzles, work through the following five cheat sheets. They contain 80% of the Python language features in 20% of the time. So they are definitely worth your time investment.

Learn them thoroughly. Try to understand every single line of code. And catapult your skills to the next level. Most Python coders neglect to invest enough time into a thorough and comprehensive understanding of the basics such as language features, data types, and language tricks. Be different and absorb the examples in each of the cheat sheets. Open up your path to become a master coder and join the top ten percent of coders.

You can download all five cheat sheets as concise

PDFs and post them to your wall until you know them by heart:

> https://blog.finxter.com/python-cheat-sheet/.

4.1 Keywords

All programming languages reserve certain words to have a special meaning. These words are called *keywords*. With keywords, the programmer can issue commands to the compiler or interpreter. They let you tell the computer what to do. Without keywords, the computer could not make sense from the seemingly random text in your code file. Note that as keywords are reserved words, you cannot use them as variable names.

The most important Python keywords are the following.

False	True	and	or
not	break	continue	class
def	if	elif	else
for	while	in	is
None	lambda	return	

The next cheat sheet introduces the most important keywords in Python. In each row, you can find the keyword itself, a short description, and an example of its usage.

Keyword	Description	Code example
False, True	Data values from the data type Boolean	```False == (1 > 2)``` ```True == (2 > 1)```

and, or,
not
	Logical operators:
	(x and y) → both x and y must be True
	(x or y) → either x or y must be True
	(not x) → x must be false
		```x, y = True, False```
		```(x or y) == True```
		```# True```
		```(x and y) == False```
		```# True```
		```(not y) == True```
		```# True```

break	Ends loop prematurely	```while(True):```
		``` break # no infinite loop```
		```print("hello world")```

continue	Finishes current loop iteration	```while(True):```
		``` continue```
		``` print("43") # dead code```

class
 	
def
	Defines a new class → a real-world concept (object oriented programming)
	
	Defines a new function or class method. For latter, first parameter **self** points to the class object. When calling class method, first parameter is implicit.
		```class Beer:```
		
		``` def __init__(self):```
		``` self.content = 1.0```
		
		``` def drink(self):```
		``` self.content = 0.0```
		
		```# constructor creates class```
		```becks = Beer()```
		
		```# empty beer bottle```
		```becks.drink()```

if, elif,	Conditional program execution: program starts	```x = int(input("your val: "))``` ```if x > 3: print("Big")```

else	with "if" branch, tries "elif" branches, and finishes with "else" branch (until one evaluates to True).	`elif x == 3: print("Medium")` `else: print("Small")`
for, while	`# For loop` `declaration` `for i in [0,1,2]:` `    print(i)`	`# While loop - same` `semantics` `j = 0` `while j < 3:` `    print(j)` `    j = j + 1`
in	Checks whether element is in sequence	`42 in [2, 39, 42] # True`
is	Checks whether both elements point to the same object	`y = x = 3` `x is y # True` `[3] is [3] # False`
None	Empty value constant	`def f():` `    x = 2` `f() is None # True`
lambda	Function with no name (anonymous)	`(lambda x: x + 3)(3) #` `returns 6`
return	Terminates function execution and passes the execution flow to the caller. An optional value after the return keyword specifies the result.	`def incrementor(x):` `    return x + 1` `incrementor(4) # returns 5`

4.2   Basic Data Types

Many programmers know basic data types as *primitive data types*. They provide the primitives on which higher-level concepts are built. A house is built from bricks. Likewise, a complex data type is built from basic data types. I introduce basic data types in the next cheat sheet and complex data types in Section 4.3.

Specifically, the next cheat sheet explains the three most important (classes of) basic data types in Python. First, the *boolean* data type encodes truth values. For example, the expression $42 > 3$ evaluates to `True` and $1 \in \{2, 4, 6\}$ evaluates to `False`. Second, the numerical types *integer*, *float*, and *complex numbers* encode integer values, floating point values, and complex values, respectively. For example, 41 is an integer value, 41.99 is a float value, and $41.999 + 0.1*i$ is a complex value (the first part of the equation being the real number and the second the imaginary number). Third, the *string* data type encodes textual data. An example of a string value is the Shakespeare quote `'Give every man thy ear, but few thy voice'`.

Data Type + Description	Example

Boolean
The Boolean data type is a truth value, either True or False.
 	
These are important Boolean operators ordered by priority (from highest to lowest):
not x →
"if x is False, then x, else y"
 	
x and y →
"if x is False, then x, else y"
 	
x or y →
"if x is False, then y, else x"
	``python
	x, y = True, False
	print(x and not y) # True
	print(not x and y or x) # True
	
	## All of those evaluate to False
	if (None or 0 or 0.0 or '' or []
	    or {} or set()):
	    print("Dead code")
	
	## All of those evaluate to True
	if (1 < 2 and 3 > 2 and 2 >=2
	    and 1 == 1 and 1 != 0):
	    print("True")
	``

Integer
An integer is a positive or negative number without floating point (e.g. 3).
 	
Float
A float is a positive or negative number with floating point precision (e.g. 3.14159265359).
 	
The '//' operator performs integer division. The result is an integer value that is rounded towards the smaller integer number (e.g. 3 // 2 == 1).
	``python
	## Arithmetic Operations
	x, y = 3, 2
	print(x + y) # = 5
	print(x - y) # = 1
	print(x * y) # = 6
	print(x / y) # = 1.5
	print(x // y) # = 1
	print(x % y) # = 1s
	print(-x) # = -3
	print(abs(-x)) # = 3
	print(int(3.9)) # = 3
	print(float(3)) # = 3.0
	print(x ** y) # = 9
	``

String
Python Strings are sequences of characters. They are immutable which means that you can not alter the characters without creating a new string.

The four main ways to create strings are the following.

1. Single quotes
```
'Yes'
```
2. Double quotes
```
"Yes"
```
3. Triple quotes (multi-line)
```
"""Yes
We Can"""
```
4. String method
```
str(5) == '5' # True
```
5. Concatenation
```
"Ma" + "hatma" #
'Mahatma'
```

These are whitespace characters in strings.
- Newline   \n
- Space   \s
- Tab   \t

```
## Indexing & Slicing
s = "The youngest pope was 11 years
old"
print(s[0])        # 'T'
print(s[1:3])      # 'he'
print(s[-3:-1])    # 'ol'
print(s[-3:])      # 'old'
x = s.split() # string array
print(x[-3] + " " + x[-1] + " " +
x[2] + "s") # '11 old popes'

## Key String Methods
y = "  This is lazy\t\n"
print(y.strip()) # 'This is lazy'
print("DrDre".lower()) # 'drdre'
print("stop".upper()) # 'STOP'
s = "smartphone"
print(s.startswith("smart")) # True
print(s.endswith("phone")) # True
print("another".find("other")) # 2
print("cheat".replace("ch", "m"))
# 'meat'
print(','.join(["F", "B", "I"]))
# 'F,B,I'
print(len("Rumpelstiltskin")) # 15
print("ear" in "earth") # True
```

4.3 Complex Data Types

In the previous section, you learned about basic data types. These are the building blocks for *complex data types*. Think of complex data types as containers—each holding a multitude of (potentially different) data types.

Specifically, the complex data types in this cheat sheet are lists, sets, and dictionaries. A list is an ordered sequence of data values (that can be either basic or complex data types). An example for such an ordered sequence is the list of all US presidents: `['Washington', 'Adams', 'Jefferson', ..., 'Obama', 'Trump']`. In contrast, a set is an *unordered* sequence of data values: `{ 'Trump', 'Washington', 'Jefferson', ..., 'Obama'}`.

Expressing the US presidents as a set loses all ordering information—it's not a sequence anymore. But sets do have an advantage over lists. Retrieving information about particular data values in the set is much faster. For instance, checking whether the string `'Obama'` is in the set of US presidents is blazingly fast even for large sets. I provide the most important methods and ideas in the following cheat sheet.

Complex Data Type + Description	Example
List A container data type that stores a sequence of elements. Unlike strings, lists are mutable: modification possible.	```l = [1, 2, 2]``` ```print(len(l)) # 3```
Adding elements to a list with append, insert, or list concatenation. The append operation is fastest.	```[1, 2, 2].append(4) # [1, 2, 2, 4]``` ```[1, 2, 4].insert(2,2) # [1, 2, 2, 4]``` ```[1, 2, 2] + [4] # [1, 2, 2, 4]```
Removing elements is slower (find it first).	```[1, 2, 2, 4].remove(1) # [2, 2, 4]```
Reversing the order of elements.	```[1, 2, 3].reverse() # [3, 2, 1]```
Sorting a list Slow for large lists: O(n log n), n list elements.	```[2, 4, 2].sort() # [2, 2, 4]```
Indexing Finds index of the first occurence of an element in the list. Is slow when traversing the whole list.	```[2, 2, 4].index(2)``` ```# index of element 4 is "0"``` ```[2, 2, 4].index(2,1)``` ```# index of el. 2 after pos 1 is "1"```
Stack Python lists can be used intuitively as stack via the two list operations append() and pop().	```stack = [3]``` ```stack.append(42) # [3, 42]``` ```stack.pop() # 42 (stack: [3])``` ```stack.pop() # 3 (stack: [])```
Set	```basket = {'apple', 'eggs',``` ``` 'banana', 'orange'}```

by comp?

Unordered collection of unique elements (*at-most-once*).	```same = set(['apple', 'eggs', 'banana', 'orange']) print(basket == same) # True``` *vgl. 2e/ set,*
Dictionary A useful data structure for storing (key, value) pairs.	```calories = {'apple' : 52, 'banana' : 89, 'choco' : 546}```
Reading and writing Read and write elements by specifying the key within the brackets. Use the keys() and values() functions to access all keys and values of the dictionary.	```c = calories print(c['apple'] < c['choco']) # True c['cappu'] = 74 print(c['banana'] < c['cappu']) # False print('apple' in c.keys()) # True print(52 in c.values()) # True```
Dictionary Looping You can access the (key, value) pairs of a dictionary with the items() method.	```for k, v in calories.items(): print(k) if v > 500 else None # 'chocolate'```
Membership operator Check with the keyword in whether the set, list, or dictionary contains an element. Set containment is faster than list containment.	```basket = {'apple', 'eggs', 'banana', 'orange'} print('eggs' in basket) # True print('mushroom' in basket) # False```
List and Set Comprehension List comprehension is the concise Python way to create lists. Use brackets plus an expression, followed by a for clause. Close with	````## List comprehension [('Hi ' + x) for x in ['Alice', 'Bob', 'Pete']] # ['Hi Alice', 'Hi Bob', 'Hi Pete'] [x * y for x in range(3) for y in range(3) if x>y]``` *Doppel!* ```# [0, 0, 2]```

| zero or more for or if clauses.

Set comprehension is similar to list comprehension. | ```
Set comprehension
squares = { x**2 for x in [0,2,4] if x < 4 } # {0, 4}
``` |

4.4 Classes

Object-oriented programming is an influential, powerful, and expressive programming abstraction. The programmer thinks in terms of classes and objects. A class is a blueprint for an object. An object contains specific data and provides the functionality specified in the class.

Say, you are programming a game to let you build, simulate, and grow cities. In object-oriented programming, you represent all things (buildings, persons, or cars) as objects. For example, each building object stores data such as name, size, and price tag. Additionally, each building provides a defined functionality such as `calculate_monthly_earnings()`. This simplifies reading and understanding your code for other programmers. Even more important, you can now easily divide responsibilities. You code the buildings and your colleague codes the moving cars.

In short, object-oriented programming helps you to write readable code. By learning object orientation, your skill of collaborating with others on complex problems improves. The next cheat sheet introduces the most basic concepts.

Description	Example

Classes
A class encapsulates data and functionality: data as attributes, and functionality as methods. It is a blueprint for creating concrete instances in memory.

	```class Dog:```
	``` """ Blueprint of a dog """```
	
	``` # class variable```
	``` # for all instances```
	``` species = ["canis lupus"]```
	
	``` def __init__(self, n, c):```
	``` self.name = n```
	``` self.state = "sleeping"```
	``` self.color = c```
	
	``` def command(self, x):```
	``` if x == self.name:```
	``` self.bark(2)```
	``` elif x == "sit":```
	``` self.state = "sit"```
	``` else:```
	``` self.state = "wag```
	``` tail"```
	
	``` def bark(self, freq):```
	``` for i in range(freq):```
	``` print(self.name```
	``` + ": Woof!")```

Instance You are an instance of the class human. An instance is a concrete implementation of a class: all attributes of an instance have a fixed value. Your hair is blond, brown, or black---but never unspecified. Each instance has its own attributes independent of other instances. Yet, class variables are different. These are data values associated with the class, not the instances. Hence, all instance share the same class variable `species` in the example.	

Self
The first argument when defining any method is always the `self` argument. This argument specifies the instance
	```bello = Dog("bello", "black")```
	```alice = Dog("alice", "white")```
	
	```print(bello.color) # black```
	```print(alice.color) # white```

on which you call the method.

self gives the Python interpreter the information about the concrete instance. To *define* a method, you use self to modify the instance attributes. But to *call* an instance method, you do not need to specify self.

```python
class Employee():
    pass
employee = Employee()
employee.salary = 122000
employee.firstname = "alice"
employee.lastname =
"wonderland"

print(employee.firstname +
" " + employee.lastname +
" $" + str(employee.salary))
# alice wonderland $122000
```

```python
bello.bark(1) # bello: Woof!

alice.command("sit")
print("alice: " +
alice.state)
# alice: sit

bello.command("no")
print("bello: " +
bello.state)
# bello: wag tail

alice.command("alice")
# alice: Woof!
# alice: Woof!

bello.species += ["wulf"]
print(len(bello.species)
    == len(alice.species))
# True (!)
```

4.5 Functions and Tricks

Python is full of extra tricks and special functionality. Learning these tricks makes you more efficient and productive. But more importantly, these tricks make programming easy and fun. In the next cheat sheet, I give you the most important ones.

ADVANCED FUNCTIONS

`map(func, iter)`
Executes the function on all elements of the iterable. Example:
`list(map(lambda x: x[0], ['red', 'green', 'blue']))`
`# Result: ['r', 'g', 'b']`

`map(func, i1, ..., ik)`
Executes the function on all k elements of the k iterables. Example:
`list(map(lambda x, y: str(x) + ' ' + y + 's' , [0, 2, 2],`
`['apple', 'orange', 'banana']))`
`# Result: ['0 apples', '2 oranges', '2 bananas']`

`string.join(iter)`
Concatenates iterable elements separated by `string`. Example:
`' marries '.join(list(['Alice', 'Bob']))`
`# Result: 'Alice marries Bob'`

`filter(func, iterable)`
Filters out elements in iterable for which function returns False (or 0). Example:
`list(filter(lambda x: True if x>17 else False, [1, 15, 17,`
`18])) # Result: [18]`

`string.strip()`
Removes leading and trailing whitespaces of string. Example:
`print("\n   \t  42  \t ".strip()) # Result: 42`

`sorted(iter)`
Sorts iterable in ascending order. Example:
`sorted([8, 3, 2, 42, 5]) # Result: [2, 3, 5, 8, 42]`

`sorted(iter, key=key)`
Sorts according to the key function in ascending order. Example:
`sorted([8, 3, 2, 42, 5], key=lambda x: 0 if x==42 else x)`
`# [42, 2, 3, 5, 8]`

`help(func)` Returns documentation of func. Example:

```
help(str.upper()) # Result: '... to uppercase.'
```

```
zip(i1, i2, ...)
```
Groups the i-th elements of iterators i1, i2, ... together. Example:
```
list(zip(['Alice', 'Anna'], ['Bob', 'Jon', 'Frank']))
# Result: [('Alice', 'Bob'), ('Anna', 'Jon')]
```

Unzip
Equal to: 1) unpack the zipped list, 2) zip the result. Example:
```
list(zip(*[('Alice', 'Bob'), ('Anna', 'Jon')]
# Result: [('Alice', 'Anna'), ('Bob', 'Jon')]
```

```
enumerate(iter)
```
Assigns a counter value to each element of the iterable. Example:
```
list(enumerate(['Alice', 'Bob', 'Jon']))
# Result: [(0, 'Alice'), (1, 'Bob'), (2, 'Jon')]
```

TRICKS

python -m http.server <P>
Want to share files between your PC and your phone? Run this command in your PC's shell. <P> is any port number between 0–65535. Type < IP address of PC>:<P> in the phone's browser. Now, you can browse the files in the PC's directory.

Read comic
```
import antigravity
```
Opens the comic series xkcd in your web browser

Zen of Python
```
import this
'...Beautiful is better than ugly. Explicit is ...'
```

Swapping variables
This is a breeze in Python. No offense, Java! Example:
```
a, b = 'Jane', 'Alice'
a, b = b, a
# Result: a = 'Alice', b = 'Jane'
```

Unpacking arguments
Use a sequence as function arguments via asterisk operator *. Use a dictionary
(key, value) via double asterisk operator **. Example:

```
def f(x, y, z):
    return x + y * z
f(*[1, 3, 4]) # 13
f(**{'z' : 4, 'x' : 1, 'y' : 3}) # 13
```

Extended Unpacking
Use unpacking for multiple assignment feature in Python. Example:

```
a, *b = [1, 2, 3, 4, 5]
# Result: a = 1, b = [2, 3, 4, 5]
```

Merge two dictionaries
Use unpacking to merge two dictionaries into a single one. Example:

```
x={'Alice' : 18}
y={'Bob' : 27, 'Ann' : 22}
z = {**x,**y}
# Result: z = {'Alice': 18, 'Bob': 27, 'Ann': 22}
```

— 5 —

Fifty Code Puzzles

In the previous chapters, we have seen the benefits of puzzle-based learning. Moreover, we have revisited the most important Python keywords, data structures, tips, and tricks. Now take your pen, fill your cup of coffee, and let's dive into the 50 code puzzles in the book. The puzzles are very basic in the beginning but will become harder and harder as you proceed with the book. Again, take your time and try to understand each and every line until you move on to the next puzzle.

5.1 Hello World

Puzzle 1

```
############################
## id 321
## Puzzle Elo 527
## Correctly solved 86 %
############################


print('hello world')
```

Puzzle 1: What is the output of this code?

Code must communicate with the outside world to have any impact. If there is no interface, it is not worth executing the code—the precious CPU power would be better spent on crypto mining.

Via the *print* function, you connect your program to the outside world. This function, as the name indicates, prints a value to the standard output.

What is the standard output? You can think of it as the environment in which your Python program lives. Your standard output is the air around you. If you shout *"Ouch!"*, every person in your environment can *read* from your standard output that you just experienced pain.

The data that is printed to the standard output is of type string. A string is a sequence of characters and is defined via each of the three following ways: via the single quote (`'`), double quote (`"`), or triple quote (`'''` and `"""`). In the puzzle, we use the single quote to define our string `'hello world'`.

Again, start with an initial rating of 1000 if you are a beginner, 1500 if you are an intermediate, and 2000 if you are an advanced Python programmer. If your solution was correct, add the respective Elo difference from the table to your current Elo number. Otherwise, subtract it from your current Elo number.

The correct solution »

```
hello world
```

Add this to your current Elo rating »

Your Elo	Correct	Incorrect
0 - 500	41	-14
500 - 1000	16	-39
1000 - 1500	8	-47
1500 - 2000	8	-47
>2000	8	-47

Your current Elo rating »

1500 + 8 = 1508

5.2   Variables and Float Division

Puzzle 2

```
############################
## id 315
## Puzzle Elo 625
## Correctly solved 91 %
############################


x = 55 / 11
print(x)
```

5.0

Puzzle 2: What is the output of this code?

The majority of people solve this puzzle correctly. The puzzle has two goals. First, it introduces the concept of variables. Python evaluates the result of the expression on the right side of the equation and stores it in the variable **x**. After defining the variable, you can access it at any point in the program code.

Second, it forces you to read code carefully by means of an interesting twist: Division always returns a floating point number. Thus, variable **x** stores the float value 5.0. The print function outputs the result as a float and not as an integer value 5. This is the source of most errors in the code. People focus too much on what they mean (semantics) and too little on how they say it (syntax). But computers are not good yet at interpreting the meaning of people. We have to talk to them in their language. So you get zero points for this puzzle if your solution was the integer value 5.

The correct solution »

    5.0

Add this to your current Elo rating »

Your Elo	Correct	Incorrect
0 - 500	43	-12
500 - 1000	21	-34
1000 - 1500	9	-46
1500 - 2000	8	-47
>2000	8	-47

Your current Elo rating »

5.3 Basic Arithmetic Operations

Puzzle 3

```
############################
## id 314
## Puzzle Elo 666
## Correctly solved 75 %
############################


x = 50 * 2 + (60 - 20) / 4
print(x)                    110.0
```

Puzzle 3: What is the output of this code?

The Python interpreter is a powerful tool. In this puzzle, it acts as a simple calculator. It takes a basic mathematical expression and calculates the result.

The syntax of expressions is straightforward: use the operators $+, -, *$ and $/$ exactly as you have learned them in school. The Python interpreter will handle basic rules such as *multiplication before addition* for you.

Note that a common mistake here is that people write the result as an integer instead of a float. This can lead to bugs in the code that are hard to find.

The correct solution »

110.0

Add this to your current Elo rating »

Your Elo	Correct	Incorrect
0 - 500	44	-11
500 - 1000	23	-32
1000 - 1500	9	-46
1500 - 2000	8	-47
>2000	8	-47

Your current Elo rating »

5.4 Comments and Strings

Puzzle 4

```
#############################
## id 313
## Puzzle Elo 691
## Correctly solved 78 %
#############################


# This is a comment
answer = 42   # the answer      2 spaces with?

# Now back to the puzzle
text = "# Is this a comment?"
print(text)
```

Puzzle 4: What is the output of this code?

This puzzle introduces two basic concepts. First, variables can hold strings. In fact, variables can hold any data type. The interpreter determines the data type of a variable at runtime. The data type of a variable can change: you can assign a string to a variable, followed by an integer. Second, comments in the code start with the hash character # and end with the start of the next line. Comments are important to improve the readability of your code.

The small twist in this puzzle is the question whether the hash character within the string literal starts a new comment. This is not the case—a comment cannot appear within a string.

There are two types of comments: block comments and inline comments. Block comments are indented to the same level as the commented code. Inline comments are separated by at least two spaces on the same line as the commented code.

The Python standard recommends to write comments as complete sentences. Moreover, the standard discourages the use of inline comments because inline comments are often unnecessary and clutter the code.

Note that according to the standard, the second comment in the puzzle is considered as bad style. Write short and conside code and do not overuse comments. Be aware, a friend of mine working at Google told me that he got critized for commenting obvious statements during the coding interview.

The correct solution »

```
# Is this a comment?
```

Add this to your current Elo rating »

Your Elo	Correct	Incorrect
0 - 500	45	-10
500 - 1000	24	-31
1000 - 1500	9	-46
1500 - 2000	8	-47
>2000	8	-47

Your current Elo rating »

5.5   Index and Concatenate Strings

Puzzle 5

```
#############################
## id 331
## Puzzle Elo 742
## Correctly solved 63 %
#############################


x = 'silent'
print(x[2] + x[1] + x[0]
      + x[5] + x[3] + x[4])
```

listn

Puzzle 5: What is the output of this code?

This puzzle introduces a powerful tool for your Python toolbox: *indexing*. Make sure you feel comfortable using it because many advanced puzzles build on your proper understanding of indexing.

In Python, you can access every character in the string by using an integer value that defines the position of the character in the string. We call this integer value an *index*.

If the string has five characters as in the example, the indices of these characters are as follows.

$$\begin{array}{lcccccc} \text{String s:} & \text{s} & \text{i} & \text{l} & \text{e} & \text{n} & \text{t} \\ \text{Index:} & 0 & 1 & 2 & 3 & 4 & 5 \end{array}$$

You can index any character using the square bracket notation [] with their respective position values. Many programming novices are confused by the fact that the first element in a sequence has index 0. Therefore, you access the first character 's' with the expression s[0] and the third character 'l' with the expression s[2].

The plus operator + is context sensitive. It calculates the mathematical sum for two given numerical values but appends strings for two given string values. For example, the expression 'a' + 'b' returns a new string 'ab'.

With this information, you are now able to determine how string s is reordered using indexing notation and the '+' operator for strings.

A small note in case you were confused. There is no separate character type in Python; a character is a string of size one.

The correct solution »

```
listen
```

Add this to your current Elo rating »

Your Elo	Correct	Incorrect
0 - 500	45	-10
500 - 1000	27	-28
1000 - 1500	10	-45
1500 - 2000	8	-47
>2000	8	-47

Your current Elo rating »

5.6 List Indexing

> **Puzzle 6**
>
> ```
> #############################
> ## id 337
> ## Puzzle Elo 745
> ## Correctly solved 91 %
> #############################
>
>
> squares = [1, 4, 9, 16, 25]
> print(squares[0])
> ```

Puzzle 6: What is the output of this code?

This puzzle introduces the simple but powerful list data structure in Python. You have to search very hard to find an algorithm that doesn't use a list. Many famous algorithms such as quicksort are based only on a single list as their core data structure.

Wikipedia defines a list as *"an abstract data type that represents a countable number of ordered values."* [1] The data type is "abstract" because you can use lists independently of the concrete data type(s) of the list elements.

---

[1] https://en.wikipedia.org/wiki/List_(abstract_data_type)

The Python way of handling lists and list access is simple and clean. Create a list by writing comma-separated values between the opening and closing square brackets.

In the Java programming language, you must use redundant natural language function calls such as `get(i)` to access a list value. In Python, this is much easier. You access the i-th element in a list `lst` with the intuitive bracket notation `lst[i]`. This notation is consistent for all compound data types such as strings and arrays.

This leads to small and repeated time savings during programming. The time savings of millions of developers add up to a strong collective argument for Python.

The correct solution »

1

Add this to your current Elo rating »

Your Elo	Correct	Incorrect
0 - 500	45	-10
500 - 1000	27	-28
1000 - 1500	10	-45
1500 - 2000	8	-47
>2000	8	-47

Your current Elo rating »

5.7 Slicing in Strings

> **Puzzle 7**
>
> ```
> ##############################
> ## id 336
> ## Puzzle Elo 778
> ## Correctly solved 72 %
> ##############################
>
>
> word = "galaxy"
> print(len(word[1:]))
> ```

Puzzle 7: What is the output of this code?

More than one out of four Finxter users cannot solve this puzzle. There are two concepts that are novel for them: the `len()` function and slicing.

The `len()` function is a handy tool to get the length of built-in Python data types such as strings, lists, dictionaries, or tuples. Learn it now and make your future life easier.

Slicing is a Python-specific concept for accessing a range of values in sequence types such as lists or strings. It is one of the most popular Python features. Understanding slicing is one of the key requirements for understanding most existing Python code bases. In other words, the time you invest now in mastering slicing will be repaid a hundredfold during your career.

The idea of slicing is simple. Use the bracket notation to access *a sequence* of elements instead of only a single element. You do this via the colon notation of `[start:end]`. This notation defines the start index (included) and the end index (excluded). Note that forgetting that the end index is always excluded in sequence operators is a very common source of bugs.

For the sake of completeness, let me quickly explain the advanced slicing notation `[start:end:step]`. The only difference to the previous notation is that it allows you to specify the step size as well. For example, the command `'python'[:5:2]` returns every second character up to the fourth character, i.e., the string `'pto'`.

The correct solution »

5

Add this to your current Elo rating »

Your Elo	Correct	Incorrect
0 - 500	46	-9
500 - 1000	29	-26
1000 - 1500	10	-45
1500 - 2000	8	-47
>2000	8	-47

Your current Elo rating »

1556

5.8   Integer Division

Puzzle 8

```
#############################
## id 316
## Puzzle Elo 781
## Correctly solved 69 %
#############################


x = 50 // 11
print(x)
```

Puzzle 8: What is the output of this code?

When I started to learn Python 3, I used to be confused about the semantics of dividing two integers. Is the result a float or an integer value? The reason for my confusion was a nasty Java bug that I once found in my code. The code was supposed to perform a simple division of two integers and return a float parameter value between zero and one. But Java uses integer division, i.e., it skips the remainder. Thus, the value was always either zero or one, but took never a value in-between. It took me days to figure that out.

Save yourself the debugging time by memorizing the following rule once and for all. The // operator performs integer (floor) division and the / operator performs float (true) division. An example for floor division is 50 // 11 = 4. An example for true division is 50 / 11 = 4.545454545454546.

Note that floor division always rounds "down", i.e., 3 // 2 == 1 and -3 // 2 == -2.

Although the puzzle seems simple, more than twenty percent of the Finxter users cannot solve it.

The correct solution »

4

Add this to your current Elo rating »

Your Elo	Correct	Incorrect
0 - 500	46	-9
500 - 1000	29	-26
1000 - 1500	10	-45
1500 - 2000	8	-47
>2000	8	-47

Your current Elo rating »   1564

5.9   String Manipulation Operators

```
#############################
## id 327
## Puzzle Elo 786
## Correctly solved 60 %
#############################


print(3 * 'un' + 'ium')
```

Puzzle 9: What is the output of this code?

Python has powerful built-in capabilities for string manipulation. Web companies like Google love Python because it is a perfect fit for the text-based World Wide Web. The puzzle explains two basic string manipulation operators. The + operator concatenates two strings. The * operator concatenates a string to itself repeatedly. The standard arithmetic rules apply to these operators: *multiplication first, then addition.*

The correct solution »

> `unununium`

Add this to your current Elo rating »

Your Elo	Correct	Incorrect
0 - 500	46	-9
500 - 1000	30	-25
1000 - 1500	10	-45
1500 - 2000	8	-47
>2000	8	-47

Your current Elo rating »   *1517*

5.10   Implicit String Concatenation

Puzzle 10

```
#############################
## id 328
## Puzzle Elo 794
## Correctly solved 74 %
#############################


x = 'py' 'thon'
print(x)
```

Puzzle 10: What is the output of this code?

A well-designed puzzle conveys one single point that surprises the reader. This puzzle introduces a language feature that surprised me when I first saw it. The Python interpreter automatically concatenates two strings that are next to each other. Think about all the pluses + you could save!

Just kidding: forget this trick immediately. Code is read much more often than it is written and these tricks will confuse some readers of your code. My editor even recommended skipping this puzzle because it may be confusing. Although he is totally right, I still keep it in the book because I think you may find it interesting—and because you may also want to understand other people's dirty code.

The correct solution »

    python

Add this to your current Elo rating »

Your Elo	Correct	Incorrect
0 - 500	46	-9
500 - 1000	30	-25
1000 - 1500	10	-45
1500 - 2000	8	-47
>2000	8	-47

Your current Elo rating »

5.11   Sum and Range Functions

```
##############################
## id 93
## Puzzle Elo 815
## Correctly solved 76 %
##############################
                              0,1,2,3,4,5,6

print(sum(range(0, 7)))
```

Puzzle 11: What is the output of this code?

Do you know the story of the brilliant mathematician Carl Friedrich Gauss? When 8-year old Gauss went to school, his math teacher sought a break. He told his class to solve the problem of adding all consecutive numbers from 1 to 100: $1 + 2 + 3 + ... + 100$. But as little Gauss promptly reported the solution, the break was over before it began. Surprised (and a bit grumpy as the story goes), the teacher asked the boy how he had come up with a solution so quickly. Gauss explained his simple solution. He organized the sequence into pairs of numbers each summing up to 101: $1 + 100, 2 + 99, 3 + 98, ..., 50 + 51$. There are 50 such pairs, so the total result was $50 * 101 = 5050$.

Yet, the modern-time little Gauss would be even lazier. He would type the following one-liner into his mobile Python app: `sum(range(1,101))`. The range function returns a sequence starting from the first value (inclusive) and ending at the second value (exclusive). The sum function sums up the values of this sequence. Combining both functions sums up the sequence from 1 100. Although your computer uses a brute-force approach, it computes the result faster than any human—dumb, but blazingly fast!

The correct solution »

21

Add this to your current Elo rating »

Your Elo	Correct	Incorrect
0 - 500	46	-9
500 - 1000	31	-24
1000 - 1500	11	-44
1500 - 2000	8	-47
>2000	8	-47

Your current Elo rating »   1533

5.12   Append Function for Lists

Puzzle 12

```
#############################
## id 341
## Puzzle Elo 821
## Correctly solved 71 %
#############################


cubes = [1, 8, 27]
cubes.append(4 ** 3)
print(cubes)
```

Puzzle 12: What is the output of this code?

This puzzle shows how you can add a new value to the end of the list using the append() function. Before appending, the Python interpreter evaluates the expression given within the brackets. Recall that the ** operator returns the power function, i.e., 4 ** 3 reads *four to the power of three.*

The correct solution »

```
[1, 8, 27, 64]
```

Add this to your current Elo rating »

Your Elo	Correct	Incorrect
0 - 500	46	-9
500 - 1000	32	-23
1000 - 1500	11	-44
1500 - 2000	8	-47
>2000	8	-47

Your current Elo rating »

154

5.13   Overshoot Slicing

Puzzle 13

```
##############################
## id 335
## Puzzle Elo 829
## Correctly solved 83 %
##############################


word = "galaxy"
print(word[4:50])
```

Puzzle 13: What is the output of this code?

This puzzle introduces a special feature of slicing. As a recap, Python slicing means to access a subsequence of a sequence type using the notation [start:end]. We show here that slicing is robust even if the end index *overshoots* the maximal sequence index. So the big take away from this puzzle is—that nothing unexpected happens if slicing overshoots sequence indices.

The correct solution »

```
xy
```

Add this to your current Elo rating »

Your Elo	Correct	Incorrect
0 - 500	46	-9
500 - 1000	32	-23
1000 - 1500	11	-44
1500 - 2000	8	-47
>2000	8	-47

Your current Elo rating »

1549

5.14   Modulo Operator

Puzzle 14

```
##############################
## id 317
## Puzzle Elo 835
## Correctly solved 62 %
##############################


x = 51 % 3
print(x)
```

Puzzle 14: What is the output of this code?

When I studied computer science, the professors pushed us to learn the theory behind modulo operations and residual classes. But many of us lacked motivation to do so. We could not see why calculating the remainder of the division, i.e., modulo, is such an important concept.

Yet, many practical code projects later, I must admit that modulo plays a role in many of them. Learning modulo is not optional. Suppose your code has a main loop and you want to execute a monitoring function each thousandth iteration i. Modulo is your friend here: simply use the fact that for every thousandth iteration, the result of i%1000 is zero.

Learning these small code patterns is the key to becoming a great coder. You must know them by heart, without much thinking. This frees your mental energy and allows you to focus on the big picture. You will produce better and more meaningful code. In fact, one of the main ideas of the website `Finxter.com` is to burn these small code patterns into your head.

The correct solution »

    0

Add this to your current Elo rating »

Your Elo	Correct	Incorrect
0 - 500	46	-9
500 - 1000	32	-23
1000 - 1500	11	-44
1500 - 2000	8	-47
>2000	8	-47

Your current Elo rating » 1557

5.15 Branching Statements

Puzzle 15

```
############################
## id 148
## Puzzle Elo 845
## Correctly solved 36 %
############################

def if_confusion(x, y):
    if x > y:
        if x - 5 > 0:
            x = y
            if y == y + y:
                return "A"
            return "B"
        elif x + y > 0:
            while x > y: x -= 1
            while y > x: y -= 1
            if x == y:
                return "E"
        else:
            x *= 2
            if x == y:
                return"F"
            return "G"
    else:
        if x - 2 > y - 4:
            x_old = x
            x = y * y
            y = 2 * x_old
            if (x - 4) ** 2 > (y - 7) ** 2:
                return "C"
            return "D"
        return "H"

print(if_confusion(3, 7))
```

Puzzle 15: What is the output of this code?

Now it is getting interesting! When I made this puzzle, I thought that it might be too simple. But look at the numbers: only 36% of our users solved it. An interesting observation is that the puzzle still has a low Elo rating. This indicates that finxters with higher Elo can solve it easily. Hence, these intermediate to advanced coders have low error rates and push it down the Elo ladder. But finxters with lower Elo ratings struggle with the puzzle.

Here are a few tips for the latter group. Never let the sheer mass of code intimidate you. You do not have to read each and every line to adhere to any kind of perfectionism. Your computer does not execute the code strictly from top to bottom and you shouldn't as well. Instead, start where the programm execution starts: at the bottom with the function call `if_confusion(3, 7)`. Now you know that `x=3` and `y=7`. Then you proceed to do what the interpreter does. As `x>y` is false, you can skip the whole upper part of the function. Similarly, you can skip the if branch for `x-2>y-4`. It's easy to see that the function returns `'H'`.

The correct solution »

```
H
```

Add this to your current Elo rating »

Your Elo	Correct	Incorrect
0 - 500	46	-9
500 - 1000	33	-22
1000 - 1500	11	-44
1500 - 2000	8	-47
>2000	8	-47

Your current Elo rating »   *1565*

5.16   Negative Indices

Puzzle 16

```
#############################
## id 332
## Puzzle Elo 848
## Correctly solved 54 %
#############################


x = 'cool'
print(x[-1] + x[-2]
      + x[-4] + x[-3])
```

Puzzle 16: What is the output of this code?

You can index single characters in strings using the bracket notation. The first character has index 0, the second index 1, and so on. Did you ever want to access the last element in a string? Counting the indices can be a real pain for long strings with more than 8–10 characters. But no worries, Python has a language feature for this. Instead of starting counting from the left, you can also start from the right. Access the *last* character with the negative index -1, the second last with the index -2, and so on. In summary, there are two ways to index sequence positions, from the left and from the right.

The correct solution »

```
loco
```

Add this to your current Elo rating »

Your Elo	Correct	Incorrect
0 - 500	46	-9
500 - 1000	33	-22
1000 - 1500	11	-44
1500 - 2000	8	-47
>2000	8	-47

Your current Elo rating »   1573

5.17   The For Loop

Puzzle 17

```
############################
## id 348
## Puzzle Elo 858
## Correctly solved 67 %
############################


words = ['cat', 'mouse']
for word in words:
    print(len(word))
```

Puzzle 17: What is the output of this code?

Repetition is everywhere. The sun goes up every morning and after winter comes spring. As coders, we model and simulate the real world and create our own worlds with our own laws and repetitions. Suppose you want to program a web server that repeats forever the following behavior. Wait for a user request and answer it. How can you program the web server to repeat this behavior thousands of times?

The naive approach is to put the sequence of steps into the source code itself. In other words, copy and paste the sequence of steps thousands of times. Yet, *repeated code* is redundant and hard to read, debug, and maintain. As programmers, we should avoid redundant code at all costs.

The Python for loop statement is a way out of redundant code. You write code only once and put it into different contexts. For example, the loop variable (i.e., word in the puzzle) accounts for the different contexts of loop executions. In the puzzle, the variable word takes first the value 'cat' and second the value 'mouse'.

Among the ingredients that make a programming language powerful are *control flow statements*. The Python for loop is one such control flow statement. It repeats execution of the code body for all sequence elements—iterating over all elements in the order of the sequence. In the puzzle, we print out the length of each word.

The correct solution »

3
5

Add this to your current Elo rating »

Your Elo	Correct	Incorrect
0 - 500	46	-9
500 - 1000	34	-21
1000 - 1500	11	-44
1500 - 2000	8	-47
>2000	8	-47

Your current Elo rating » 1581

5.18 Functions and Naming

Puzzle 18

```
#############################
## id 358
## Puzzle Elo 899
## Correctly solved 61 %
#############################


def func(x):
    return x + 1

f = func
print(f(2) + func(2))
```

Puzzle 18: What is the output of this code?

Too much redundant code indicates poor programming style. So how to avoid redundant code? Use *functions*. Functions make code more general. Suppose you want to calculate the square root of 145. You could either calculate it for the specific value 145 or define a function that calculates the square root for any value x.

We say that a function *encapsulates* a sequence of program instructions. The ideal function solves a single semantic high-level goal. For instance, you can encapsulate a complex task into a function, such as searching the web for specific keywords. In this way, the complex task becomes a simple one-liner: calling the function. Functions enable others to reuse your code and allow you to reuse other people's code. You are standing on the shoulders of giants.

You can define a function with the keyword `def`, followed by a name and the arguments of the function. The Python interpreter maintains a *symbol table* that stores all function definitions, i.e., mappings from function *names* to function *objects*. In this way, the interpreter can relate each occurrence of the function name to the defined function object. Just remember: a single function object can have zero, one, or even many names.

In the puzzle, we assign the function object to the name `func` and then reassign it to the new name `f`. We then use both the names in the code. Upon the function call, the Python interpreter will find the function in the symbol table and execute it. This can make your code more readable when calling the same function in different contexts.

The correct solution »

6

Add this to your current Elo rating »

Your Elo	Correct	Incorrect
0 - 500	47	-8
500 - 1000	36	-19
1000 - 1500	12	-43
1500 - 2000	8	-47
>2000	8	-47

Your current Elo rating »

1583

5.19   Concatenating Slices

Puzzle 19

```
##############################
## id 334
## Puzzle Elo 954
## Correctly solved 45 %
##############################


word = "galaxy"
print(word[:-2] + word[-2:])
```

Puzzle 19: What is the output of this code?

This puzzle revisits the important concept of slicing. Slicing is one of the most popular features in Python. Understand the term and concept of slicing and you are at least among the intermediate Python programmers.

Slicing, like indexing, retrieves specific characters from a sequence such as a string. But while indexing retrieves only a single character, slicing retrieves a whole substring within an index range.

Use the bracket notation for slicing with the start and end position identifiers. For example, `word[i:j]` returns the substring starting from index `i` (included) and ending in index j (excluded).

You can also skip the position identifier before or after the slicing colon. This indicates that the slice starts from the first or last position, respectively. For example, `word[:i] + word[i:]` returns the same string as `word`.

The correct solution »

    galaxy

Add this to your current Elo rating »

Your Elo	Correct	Incorrect
0 - 500	47	-8
500 - 1000	38	-17
1000 - 1500	14	-41
1500 - 2000	8	-47
>2000	8	-47

Your current Elo rating »   *1542*

5.20   Arbitrary Arguments

Puzzle 20

```
#############################
## id 365
## Puzzle Elo 1005
## Correctly solved 57 %
#############################

def func(a, *args):
    print(a)
    for arg in args:
        print(arg)

func("A", "B", "C")
```

Puzzle 20: What is the output of this code?

Suppose you want to create a function that allows an arbitrary number of arguments. An example is recognizing faces in images where each image consists of one or more pixel arrays. You achieve this by prefixing the function argument with the asterisk operator (or star operator), e.g., *pixels. Now, you can pass a tuple or a list as a function argument, which you can access via indexing or iteration in a loop.

You can combine both types of parameters in a function: normal positional parameters (e.g., a in the puzzle) and an arbitrary length parameter list (e.g., *args in the puzzle). If you call the function with many arguments, the interpreter fills in name slot(s) for normal positional arguments first. The arbitrary argument list handles the rest of the arguments.

The correct solution »

A

B

C

Add this to your current Elo rating »

Your Elo	Correct	Incorrect
0 - 500	47	-8
500 - 1000	40	-15
1000 - 1500	15	-40
1500 - 2000	8	-47
>2000	8	-47

Your current Elo rating »

5.21   Indirect Recursion

```
#############################
## id 76
## Puzzle Elo 1032
## Correctly solved 54 %
#############################


def ping(i):
    if i > 0:
        return pong(i - 1)
    return "0"

def pong(i):
    if i > 0:
        return ping(i - 1)
    return "1"

print(ping(29))
```

Puzzle 21: What is the output of this code?

Recursion is a powerful tool in your coding toolbox. Understanding it is a key skill on your path to mastery. So what is recursion? Stephen Hawking used a concise explanation: *"to understand recursion, one must first understand recursion."*

This puzzle uses indirect recursion: function f calls function g which calls function f. Each function call solves a slightly easier problem. In recursive problem solving, a function knows the result for some base cases (i.e., the naive solutions). It breaks a complex problem into a combination of less complex subproblems. As the subproblems are getting easier, they finally reach the base cases. These are the least complex subproblems and we know their solutions. The idea is to build the solution of the complex problem from the solutions of the subproblems.

So when you call ping(29), the ping function reduces this question to pong(28)—an easier problem. The calling function ping waits for pong to return a solution. But pong asks back ping(27) and waits for a solution. On a higher level, ping receives odd and pong even argument values for the initial input i=29. Thus, the last call is pong(0), which returns 1. Each calling function is waiting for the result of the called function. Each calling function receives the value 1 and returns it to its parent calling function. Finally, the top-most functional instance ping(29) returns the value 1 as the final result.

The correct solution »

1

Add this to your current Elo rating »

Your Elo	Correct	Incorrect
0 - 500	47	-8
500 - 1000	41	-14
1000 - 1500	16	-39
1500 - 2000	8	-47
>2000	8	-47

Your current Elo rating »

5.22 String Slicing

```
############################
## id 333
## Puzzle Elo 1038
## Correctly solved 53 %
############################


word = "bender"
print(word[1:4])      end
```

Puzzle 22: What is the output of this code?

The language feature slicing does not only apply to lists, but also to strings. As both lists and strings are sequencing types, slicing is only one among several similarities. For example, you can also iterate over the characters in a string using the for loop (e.g., `for c in word`).

Only half of the Finxter users can solve this puzzle. The main problem is to identify the correct end index of the slice. Recap: the end index is not included in the slice. Here is how you can find the correct solution (in bold).

b	e	n	d	e	r
0	1	2	3	4	5

The correct solution »

    end

Add this to your current Elo rating »

Your Elo	Correct	Incorrect
0 - 500	47	-8
500 - 1000	41	-14
1000 - 1500	17	-38
1500 - 2000	8	-47
>2000	8	-47

Your current Elo rating »

5.23 Slice Assignment

```
############################
## id 342
## Puzzle Elo 1104
## Correctly solved 52 %
############################



customers = ['Marie', 'Anne', 'Donald']
customers[2:4] = ['Barack', 'Olivia', 'Sophia']
print(customers)
```

Puzzle 23: What is the output of this code?

A great coder seeks the cleanest and shortest way to accomplish their goals. This puzzle demonstrates a Python trick that I found very useful: *slice assignments*.

Suppose you work in a biotech startup on DNA sequence modeling. You maintain different DNA sequences as lists of string values. To simulate recombinations of DNA sequences, you change subsequences of the list on a regular basis. In this case, slicing is your best friend: It helps you to read specific subsequences. Moreover, slice assignments enable you to replace, append, or clear whole subsequences.

In the puzzle, we have a list of customers that are partially replaced by new customers. The puzzle shows how the length of the original sequence may change due to the slice assignment. The slice assignment inserts a list of three customers into the customer list. A beautiful way to clear the list is: `customers[:] = []`.

The correct solution »

> ['Marie', 'Anne', 'Barack', 'Olivia', 'Sophia']

Add this to your current Elo rating »

Your Elo	Correct	Incorrect
0 - 500	47	-8
500 - 1000	43	-12
1000 - 1500	20	-35
1500 - 2000	8	-47
>2000	8	-47

Your current Elo rating »   *1517*

5.24 Default Arguments

Puzzle 24

```
############################
## id 360
## Puzzle Elo 1152
## Correctly solved 50 %
############################


def ask(prompt, retries=4, output='Error'):
    for _ in range(retries):
        response = input(prompt).lower()
        if response in ['y', 'yes']:
            return True
        if response in ['n', 'no']:
            return False
        print(output)


print(ask('Want to know the answer?', 5))
```

Puzzle 24: Is `ask('Want to know the answer?', 5)` a valid function call?

This puzzle introduces the concept of default arguments in Python.

Suppose you have created a Python command line

tool for your business. The tool requires user confirmation for different activities like writing or deleting files.

To avoid redundant code, you have implemented a generic function that handles the interaction with the user. The default behavior should consist of three steps: (1) You ask (prompt) the user a yes/no question; (2) the user enters some response; (3) as long as the response is invalid, the function repeats up to four times—each time printing an error message 'Error'. The number of repetitions and the reminder should be customizable via the parameters.

To achieve this, you can specify default arguments as given in the puzzle. You can use the default parameters by calling `ask('Hi?')`. Or you can overwrite them in the order of their definition (one, several, or all parameters).

Also did you notice that single underscore is a valid name in Python? By convention, you can use it as a throw-away name—when you don't really need to access the actual value. In the puzzle, we ask the user four times but do not need to know how often we have *already* asked.

It is interesting that only 50% of all Finxter users solve this puzzle correctly. That's no better than random guessing. Partial replacement of default arguments is a new feature to most users. Is it new to you? You have to master these basic language features before you can climb to the level of an advanced coder.

The correct solution »

    Yes

Add this to your current Elo rating »

Your Elo	Correct	Incorrect
0 - 500	47	-8
500 - 1000	44	-11
1000 - 1500	22	-33
1500 - 2000	9	-46
>2000	8	-47

Your current Elo rating »

5.25   Slicing and the `len()` Function

Puzzle 25

```
############################
## id 344
## Puzzle Elo 1211
## Correctly solved 44 %
############################


letters = ['a', 'b', 'c', 'd']
print(len(letters[1:-1]))
```

Puzzle 25: What is the output of this code?

The goal of this puzzle is to deepen your understanding of the important concept of slicing.

Yet, it turned out to be more a test of thoroughness than anything else. The majority of users cannot solve this puzzle—one of the most common errors is to overlook the word `len()`.

The built-in function `len()` returns the length of a sequence object such as a string or a list. In the puzzle, we return the length of the list after cutting the head and the tail. An illuminating example for lack of thoroughness, which is also the major source of bugs in your code. Ask any professional programmer!

The correct solution »

> 2

Add this to your current Elo rating »

Your Elo	Correct	Incorrect
0 - 500	47	-8
500 - 1000	45	-10
1000 - 1500	25	-30
1500 - 2000	9	-46
>2000	8	-47

Your current Elo rating »

5.26   Nested Lists

Puzzle 26

```
##############################
## id 345
## Puzzle Elo 1238
## Correctly solved 39 %
##############################


a = ['a', 'b']
n = [1, 2]
x = [a, n]
print(x[1])
```

Puzzle 26: What is the output of this code?

Many practical code projects use lists containing not only primitive but also complex data types. Examples of primitive data types are integers, strings, or floats. Examples of complex data types are customer objects, camera events, or even lists.

In the puzzle, we show the latter: there is a nested list that contains two other lists. Accessing an element of this list using the index notation returns a list itself.

Python is a dynamically typed programming language. Hence, there can be hybrid lists containing different data types. However, this is not too common.

The correct solution »

    [1, 2]

Add this to your current Elo rating »

Your Elo	Correct	Incorrect
0 - 500	47	-8
500 - 1000	45	-10
1000 - 1500	27	-28
1500 - 2000	9	-46
>2000	8	-47

Your current Elo rating »   1548

5.27　Clearing Sublists

Puzzle 27

```
############################
## id 343
## Puzzle Elo 1248
## Correctly solved 47 %
############################


letters = ['a', 'b', 'c',
           'd', 'e', 'f', 'g']
letters[1:] = []
print(letters)
```

Puzzle 27: What is the output of this code?

In verbose programming languages such as Java, you have to iterate over a list to remove subsequent elements. In Python, a simple one-liner does that for you. Use the slice notation to select a sequence of items in the list. This is the lefthand side of your equation. Then overwrite the selected sequence with the empty (or any other) list. It is because of this kind of clarity and simplicity that Python has become so popular nowadays.

The correct solution »

> ['a']

Add this to your current Elo rating »

Your Elo	Correct	Incorrect
0 - 500	47	-8
500 - 1000	45	-10
1000 - 1500	27	-28
1500 - 2000	10	-45
>2000	8	-47

Your current Elo rating »

5.28   The Fibonacci Series

Puzzle 28

```
##############################
## id 346
## Puzzle Elo 1300
## Correctly solved 48 %
##############################


# Fibonacci series:
a, b = 0, 1
while b < 5:
    print(b)
    a, b = b, a + b
```

Puzzle 28: What is the output of this code?

The Fibonacci series was discovered by the Italian mathematician Leonardo Fibonacci in 1202 and even earlier by Indian mathematicians. The series appears in unexpected areas such as economics, mathematics, art, and nature.

In the puzzle, we give a simple algorithm to calculate the Fibonacci numbers. The series starts with the Fibonacci numbers zero and one. The algorithm calculates the next element of the series as the sum of the previous two elements. For this, the algorithm only has to keep track of the last two elements in the series. Thus, we maintain two variables a and b, being the second last and last element in the series, respectively. This computation repeats until the while condition evaluates to False, i.e., until b$\geq$5.

For clarity of the code, I used the language feature of *iterable unpacking* in the first and the last line. This feature works as follows. On the left-hand side of the assignment, there is any sequence of variables. On the right-hand side of the assignment, we specify the values to be assigned to these variables.

Note that all expressions on the right-hand side are first evaluated before they are assigned. This is an important property for our algorithm. Without this property, the last line would be wrong as the expression a+b would consider the wrong value for a.

The correct solution »

1 1 2 3

Add this to your current Elo rating »

Your Elo	Correct	Incorrect
0 - 500	47	-8
500 - 1000	46	-9
1000 - 1500	30	-25
1500 - 2000	10	-45
>2000	8	-47

Your current Elo rating »

5.29   The `continue` Statement and the Modulo Operator

Puzzle 29

```
#############################
## id 355
## Puzzle Elo 1311
## Correctly solved 54 %
#############################

for num in range(2, 8):
    if not num % 2:
        continue
    print(num)
```

Puzzle 29: What is the output of this code?

This puzzle prints all odd values between two (included) and eight (excluded). To achieve this, we check whether the current value `num` can be divided by 2 without remainder. Python, like other languages, uses the percentage symbol `%` as modulo operator. This modulo operator returns the remainder when dividing a number `n` by another number `x`, i.e., `n - (n//x) * x`. For example, it returns `12 % 2 = 0` if there is no remainder and `13 % 2 = 1` if the remainder is 1.

There is a second language feature in the puzzle, which is the `continue` operator. This operator commands the interpreter to terminate the current loop iteration. Then, the interpreter proceeds with the next iteration.

Hence, if the loop variable has an even value, the interpreter skips the print statement. If the loop variable has an odd value, the interpreter skips the continue statement.

The correct solution »

```
3
5
7
```

Add this to your current Elo rating »

Your Elo	Correct	Incorrect
0 - 500	47	-8
500 - 1000	46	-9
1000 - 1500	31	-24
1500 - 2000	10	-45
>2000	8	-47

Your current Elo rating »

1464

1481

5.30 Indexing Revisited and The Range Sequence

Puzzle 30

```
#############################
## id 351
## Puzzle Elo 1346
## Correctly solved 52 %
#############################

print(range(5, 10)[-1])          9
print(range(0, 10, 3)[2])        6
print(range(-10, -100, -30)[1])   -40
```

Puzzle 30: What is the output of this code?

If this book can teach you only one thing, it is a thorough understanding of the most important Python concepts such as indexing and slicing. I cannot emphasize enough how important these concepts are for your practical work. The goal of this puzzle is to strengthen your understanding of these. The puzzle consists of three quick tasks about indexing and the range function. Repetition is an effective teacher!

The first line prints the last element of the range sequence. A short reminder: the upper bound range parameter is not included in the sequence. The second line prints the third element (not the second) of the range sequence 0, 3, 6, 9. Thus, the step size is three as defined in the last optional range parameter. The third line prints the second element of the range sequence -10, -40, -70 with step size -30.

Many finxters have problems with indexing or the range function. One common mistake is that they select the wrong element from the sequence—forgetting that the first element of any sequence has index 0, not index 1.

It is the proficient use of the basics that differentiates excellent from average programmers.

The correct solution »

9

6

-40

Add this to your current Elo rating »

Your Elo	Correct	Incorrect
0 - 500	47	-8
500 - 1000	46	-9
1000 - 1500	33	-22
1500 - 2000	11	-44
>2000	8	-47

Your current Elo rating »

5.31 Searching in Sorted Matrix

Puzzle 31

```
#############################
## id 112
## Puzzle Elo 1353
## Correctly solved 41 %
#############################


def matrix_find(matrix, value):
    if not matrix or not matrix[0]:
        return False

    j = len(matrix) - 1
    for row in matrix:
        while row[j] > value:
            j = j - 1
            if j == -1:
                return False
        if row[j] == value:
            return True
    return False

matrix = [[3, 4, 4, 6],
          [6, 8, 11, 12],
          [6, 8, 11, 15],
          [9, 11, 12, 17]]
print(matrix_find(matrix=matrix, value=11))
```

Puzzle 31: What is the output of this code?

The puzzles are getting harder now. The challenge is shifting from understanding syntactical to semantical code snippets and algorithms. If you thoroughly master these types of code puzzles, you will join the club of advanced coders. Thus, you open up the opportunity to work in one of the highest paid job industries in the world.

This algorithm is a beautiful way to search a value in a sorted matrix without visiting all values. In the next paragraph, I describe the matrix concept and the sorted property.

A matrix is a table of values consisting of rows and columns. This puzzle represents it as a list of integer lists. Hence, we can access matrix values with the indexing and slicing notation. Do you see the importance of understanding the basics? The matrix is *sorted* as the integers in the rows and columns increase monotonically with the row and column number.

The function `matrix_find` takes a sorted integer matrix and an integer value. It returns `True` if the matrix contains the integer value. Otherwise, it returns `False`.

In the first two lines, the algorithm checks whether the matrix is empty and returns `False` if this is the case. Then, the for loop iterates over rows of the matrix starting with the first row.

But instead of searching the whole matrix, the algorithm uses a smarter strategy. It skips whole rows and columns at a time using the sorted property.

The algorithm starts with the first row and the last column j = len(matrix) - 1. Then, it skips one column at-a-time by decreasing the parameter j monotonically (j = j - 1). Why can it skip the whole column? Because as long as the column value row[j] is larger than the searched value **value**, all following elements of column j are larger than the searched value (sorted property). Thus, we are sure that our searched value is not in column j and we can skip this column completely by decreasing j.

If the column value row[j] is smaller than the searched value, the algorithm skips this whole row by going to the next row. Why can it skip the whole row? Because it currently checks the largest value in the row. If this value is smaller than the searched value, all other values are as well.

In summary, the idea of this great algorithm from Keith Schwartz[2] is to skip either one row or one column in each step. Thus, for a quadratic matrix with n rows and columns, the algorithm inspects approximately $2n$ cells. Note that a naive algorithm would inspect all n^2 cells which is much slower.

---

[2]http://www.keithschwarz.com/interesting/code/matrix-find/MatrixFind.python.html

The correct solution »

    True

Add this to your current Elo rating »

Your Elo	Correct	Incorrect
0 - 500	47	-8
500 - 1000	46	-9
1000 - 1500	33	-22
1500 - 2000	11	-44
>2000	8	-47

Your current Elo rating »

5.32 Maximum Profit Algorithm

Puzzle 32

```
#############################
## id 36
## Puzzle Elo 1407
## Correctly solved 65 %
#############################


def maximum_profit(prices):
    '''Maximum profit of a single buying low and
    ↪  selling high'''

    profit = 0
    for i, buy_price in enumerate(prices):
        sell_price = max(prices[i:])
        profit = max(profit, sell_price -
        ↪  buy_price)
    return profit

# Ethereum daily prices in Dec 2017 ($)
eth_prices = [455, 460, 465, 451, 414, 415, 441]
print(maximum_profit(prices=eth_prices))
```

Puzzle 32: What is the output of this code?

This puzzle presents an algorithmic problem with practical value for stock market analysis. Suppose you are trading the cryptocurrency Ethereum. How much profit can you make by buying low and selling high based on historical data?

The function `maximum_profit` takes as input a sequence of prices, e.g., a week of Ethereum prices in December 2017. It returns the largest possible profit of buying low and selling high.

The algorithm works as follows. It iterates over all sequence values: each is a possible buying point (i.e., `buy_price`). Note that the enumerate function returns both the index `i` of the next price in the sequence and the price itself.

Next, the algorithm uses the index `i` of the current buying point to get all potential selling points after buying. We use slicing to get these, i.e., `prices[i:]`. The max function finds the highest selling point. For each buying/selling pair (`buy_price, sell_price`), it calculates the profit as the difference between the prices at the selling and the buying points, i.e., `sell_price-buy_price`. The variable `profit` maintains the largest possible profit: $27 on $414 invested capital.

The correct solution »

27

Add this to your current Elo rating »

Your Elo	Correct	Incorrect
0 - 500	47	-8
500 - 1000	47	-8
1000 - 1500	36	-19
1500 - 2000	12	-43
>2000	8	-47

Your current Elo rating »

1537

5.33   Bubble Sort Algorithm

Puzzle 33

```
############################
## id 158
## Puzzle Elo 1458
## Correctly solved 67 %
############################


def bubble_sort(lst):
    '''Implementation of bubble sort
    ↪   algorithm'''

    for border in range(len(lst)-1, 0, -1):
        for i in range(border):
            if lst[i] > lst[i + 1]:
                lst[i], lst[i + 1] = lst[i + 1],
                ↪   lst[i]
    return lst

list_to_sort = [27, 0, 71, 70, 27, 63, 90]
print(bubble_sort(lst=list_to_sort))
```

Puzzle 33: What is the output of this code?

The bubble sort algorithm works exactly as its name suggests. It sorts an input list by treating each element as a bubble that climbs up the list. Each bubble rises as long as it is greater than the list elements. If the bubble element is smaller or equal than a list element x, the bubble stops rising, and the larger list element x starts to bubble up.

The precise algorithm works as follows. The outer index variable **border** marks the index after which the right-hand list elements are already sorted. The inner index variable i goes from left to right until it reaches the index variable **border**. On its way to the right, it switches two subsequent list elements if the first element is larger than the second element. Hence, after the first pass, the largest element in the list is on the right. As this right-most element is already sorted, we can reduce the size of the list to be sorted by one—i.e., decrement the variable **border**. Next, the second largest element will rise to the top and the procedure repeats.

Study this basic algorithm carefully. Every great coder must know it.

The correct solution »

```
[0, 27, 27, 63, 70, 71, 90]
```

Add this to your current Elo rating »

Your Elo	Correct	Incorrect
0 - 500	47	-8
500 - 1000	47	-8
1000 - 1500	38	-17
1500 - 2000	14	-41
>2000	8	-47

Your current Elo rating »

1571

5.34 Joining Strings

Puzzle 34

```
############################
## id 367
## Puzzle Elo 1437
## Correctly solved 53 %
############################

def concatenation(*args, sep="/"):
    return sep.join(args)

print(concatenation("A", "B", "C", sep=","))
```

Puzzle 34: What is the output of this code?

 A,B,C

String concatenation is the process of creating a string by appending string arguments. The given function takes an arbitrary number of string arguments as specified by the *args keyword. The parameter sep declares the separator string to be used to glue together two strings. The separator string comes as a keyword argument. The reason is that the *args argument comprises an arbitrary number of values. The keyword argument helps to differentiate whether the last parameter is part of *args or the sep argument.

The function `concatenation` is a wrapper for the join function to concatenate strings. The join function is defined in the string object `sep`. It concatenates an arbitrary number of strings using the separator to glue them together. Both functions achieve the same thing, but the first may be more convenient because the separator is a normal argument. Yet, you will find yourself using the join function on a regular basis without writing your own wrapper functions. So you may as well learn its proper use now.

The correct solution »

    A,B,C

Add this to your current Elo rating »

Your Elo	Correct	Incorrect
0 - 500	47	-8
500 - 1000	47	-8
1000 - 1500	37	-18
1500 - 2000	13	-42
>2000	8	-47

Your current Elo rating »

5.35 Arithmetic Calculations

Puzzle 35

```
#############################
## id 320
## Puzzle Elo 1486
## Correctly solved 7 %
#############################

x = 5 * 3.8 - 1
print(x)
```

Puzzle 35: What is the output of this code?

This puzzle has only one challenge. But this challenge is so hard that only 7% of all finxters can overcome it: floating point operators.

Most finxters believe that the puzzle asks for the result of the computation here. But this is a trap! The purpose of solving Python puzzles is to understand code in a precise and deep manner. Deep understanding tells you that the float 3.80 causes the interpreter to perform floating point arithmetic. Thus, the result is not an integer—i.e., the value 18—but a float—i.e., the value 18.0.

These kinds of mistakes seem to be negligible but they

have important effects on the correctness of your code base. So if you got this puzzle wrong, be grateful for the lesson and go on.

The correct solution »

    18.0

Add this to your current Elo rating »

Your Elo	Correct	Incorrect
0 - 500	47	-8
500 - 1000	47	-8
1000 - 1500	39	-16
1500 - 2000	15	-40
>2000	8	-47

Your current Elo rating »

1575

5.36 Binary Search

Puzzle 36

```
#############################
id 159
## Puzzle Elo 1492
## Correctly solved 33 %
#############################

def bsearch(l, value):
    lo, hi = 0, len(l)-1
    while lo <= hi:
        mid = (lo + hi) // 2
        if l[mid] < value:
            lo = mid + 1
        elif value < l[mid]:
            hi = mid - 1
        else:
            return mid
    return -1


l = [0, 1, 2, 3, 4, 5, 6]
x = 6
print(bsearch(l,x))
```

Puzzle 36: What is the output of this code?

How to find a value in a sorted list? The naive algorithm compares each element in the list against the searched value. For example, consider a list with 1024 elements. The naive algorithm performs 1024 comparisons in the worst case.

The function bsearch is a more effective way to find a value in a sorted list. For n elements in the list, it needs to perform only in the order of $log(n)$ comparisons. Hence, a list with 1024 elements would take Bsearch only up to $log(1024) = 10$ comparisons—making it much faster

Why is Bsearch so fast? Bsearch uses the property that the list is already sorted. It checks only the element in the middle position between two indices `lo` and `hi`. If this middle element is smaller than the searched value, all left-hand elements will be smaller as well because of the sorted list. The algorithm can skip all left-hand elements by setting the lower index `lo` to the position right of the middle element. If this middle element is larger than the searched value, all right-hand elements will be larger as well. Hence, we set the upper index `hi` to the position left of the middle element. Only if the middle element is exactly the same as the searched value, we return the index of this position. This procedure is repeated until we find the searched value or there are no values left. In each loop iteration, we reduce the search space, i.e., the number of elements between `lo` and `hi`, by half.

The correct solution »

6

Add this to your current Elo rating »

Your Elo	Correct	Incorrect
0 - 500	47	-8
500 - 1000	47	-8
1000 - 1500	40	-15
1500 - 2000	15	-40
>2000	8	-47

Your current Elo rating »

1594

5.37 Modifying Lists in Loops

Puzzle 37

```
#############################
## id 349
## Puzzle Elo 1504
## Correctly solved 58 %
#############################

words = ['cat', 'mouse', 'dog']
for word in words[:]:
    if len(word) > 3:
        words.insert(0, word)
print(words[0])          mouse
```

Puzzle 37: What is the output of this code?

How to modify a sequence while iterating over it? For example, you want to prepare a data set of house prices for a machine learning algorithm to predict the market prices of new houses. Your goal is to remove the data points with prices lower than $20,000 to clean the data of outliers.

This problem is not as simple as removing elements from a sequence over which you iterate. Doing this can lead to unspecified behavior as explained in the following. Before entering the for loop, the Python interpreter creates an iterator object. The iterator object provides a method **next()** returning the next element in the sequence. To achieve this, the iterator extracts, at creation time, information like the size of the sequence. If you modify the sequence "on the go", this information becomes invalid. For example, if the number of elements changes at runtime, the iterator object may believe it is ready, while there are still objects in it.

The puzzle presents one solution to this problem. The code copies the list first and iterates over the copy. With this method, you can safely modify the original list as this will not affect the copy in any way.

So how to copy the sequence? The most convenient way to achieve this is by using the slice notation as shown in the puzzle.

The correct solution »

```
mouse
```

Add this to your current Elo rating »

Your Elo	Correct	Incorrect
0 - 500	47	-8
500 - 1000	47	-8
1000 - 1500	40	-15
1500 - 2000	15	-40
>2000	8	-47

Your current Elo rating »

1609

5.38 The Lambda Function

Puzzle 38

```
#############################
## id 370
## Puzzle Elo 1558
## Correctly solved 89 %
#############################

def make_incrementor(n):
    return lambda x: x + n

f = make_incrementor(42)
print(f(0))
print(f(1))
```

Puzzle 38: What is the output of this code?

This puzzle introduces an advanced language feature: lambda functions. Lambda functions are rooted in the mathematical area of lambda calculus. One of the pioneers of this area was Alonzo Church. He introduced lambda functions in 1936 even before the appearance of the first computers.

Lambda functions exist in a wide range of languages for functional programming. They are not only at the heart of functional programming languages, they are also the basis of many advanced Python language features. For example, the modern language Scala for parallel programming combines traditional language elements (e.g., from Java) with functional elements (e.g., lambda functions). So how do lambda functions work?

A lambda function is an anonymous function without identifier. After the lambda keyword, the function takes one or more arbitrary arguments. The arguments are comma-separated and finished by a colon. After the colon follows a single expression. Yet, this expression can consist of complex calculations using the specified argument variables. The lambda function then returns the result of this expression. Hence, lambda functions are syntactical shortcuts for a subclass of normal Python functions.

In the puzzle, the function `make_incrementor` creates a lambda function at runtime. The created lambda function increases an element `x` by a fixed value `n`. For example, the incrementor function in the puzzle increments a value by 42. We assign this function to the variable `f`. Then we print the results when incrementing the values 0 and 1 by the incrementor 42.

The correct solution »

42

43

Add this to your current Elo rating »

Your Elo	Correct	Incorrect
0 - 500	47	-8
500 - 1000	47	-8
1000 - 1500	42	-13
1500 - 2000	17	-38
>2000	8	-47

Your current Elo rating »

1623

5.39   Multi-line Strings and the New-line Character

Puzzle 39

```
#############################
## id 325
## Puzzle Elo 1623
## Correctly solved 71 %
#############################


print("""
A
B
C
""" == "\nA\nB\nC\n")
```

Puzzle 39: What is the output of this code?

What is going on in this puzzle? The basic idea is to show two different ways of writing the same multi-line string literal in Python.

The first is the direct way to write a multi-line string in Python: As a string with multiple code lines enclosed by triple-quotes ' ' ' . . . ' ' ' or """. . ."""".

The second is a more concise way to write the same

string. We specify the line breaks with the new line character '\n'.

These two ways of breaking lines in Python strings are the basis for advanced features and code snippets.

The correct solution »

    True

Add this to your current Elo rating »

Your Elo	Correct	Incorrect
0 - 500	47	-8
500 - 1000	47	-8
1000 - 1500	43	-12
1500 - 2000	20	-35
>2000	9	-46

Your current Elo rating »

1649

5.40   Escaping

Puzzle 40

```
#############################
## id 323
## Puzzle Elo 1629
## Correctly solved 25 %
#############################


print('P"yt\'h"on')
```

Puzzle 40: What is the output of this code?

This puzzle introduces several Python language features about quotes in string literals. It requires a clear understanding of the concept of escaping. Escaping is an important concept in most programming languages. You are not an advanced coder without understanding at least the basic idea of escaping.

Recap, strings can be enclosed either with single quotes '...' or double quotes "...". These two options are semantically equivalent, i.e., they do the same thing.

But what happens if you write, say, a small conversation with direct speech?

```
"Alice said:   "Hey Bob!" and went on."
```
(wrong)

The double quotes cannot be a part of a string en-closed in double quotes. Trying this ends the string pre-maturely. Here, the best case is that the interpreter com-plains about the strange syntax of the random character sequence after the premature ending of your string.

Yet, there is an easy fix. You can avoid this problem by enclosing the string with single quotes:

```
'Alice said:   "Hey Bob!" and went on.'
```
(right)

The double quotes can now be part of the string itself without ending the string sequence. The opposite also works, i.e., writing a single quote within a string enclosed in double quotes.

So far so good. But there is still one question left that is also the main reason why only 25% of finxters can solve this puzzle: escaping. What if you want to put a single quote within a string enclosed by single quotes?

In the puzzle, we solve this using the escape character: the backslash \. When put before special characters like the single quote, it escapes them. In other words, it changes the meaning of these characters. For example, the single quote has the meaning of starting or ending a string. Only when escaped, the interpreter changes its meaning to the normal single quote character.

The correct solution »

```
P"yt'h"on
```

Add this to your current Elo rating »

Your Elo	Correct	Incorrect
0 - 500	47	-8
500 - 1000	47	-8
1000 - 1500	43	-12
1500 - 2000	21	-34
>2000	9	-46

Your current Elo rating »

1670

5.41 Fibonacci Arithmetic

Puzzle 41

```
##############################
## id 359
## Puzzle Elo 1661
## Correctly solved 60 %
##############################


def fibo(n):
    """Return list containing
    Fibonacci series up to n.
    """

    result = []
    a, b = 0, 1
    while a < n:
        result.append(a)
        a, b = b, a + b
    return result

fib100 = fibo(100)
print(fib100[-1] ==
      fib100[-2] + fib100[-3])
```

True

Puzzle 41: What is the output of this code?

Recap the Fibonacci series is the series of numbers that arises when repeatedly summing up the last two

0 1 1 2 3 5

numbers starting from 0 and 1. The `fibo` function in the puzzle calculates all Fibonacci numbers up to the function argument **n**. We use the concise method of *iterable unpacking* to store the value of b in the variable a and to calculate the new value of b as the sum of both. We maintain the whole sequence in the list variable `result` by appending the sequence value a to the end of the list.

The puzzle calculates the Fibonacci sequence up to 100 and stores the whole list in the variable `fib100`. But to solve the puzzle, you do not have to calculate the whole sequence. The print statement only compares whether the last element is equal to the sum of the second and third last element in the sequence. This is true by definition of the Fibonacci series.

Humans can solve this puzzle easily using logic and strategic thinking. The Python interpreter, however, must take the brute-force approach of calculating everything from scratch. This nicely demonstrates your role as a computer programmer. You are the guiding hand with unlimited power at your fingertips. But you must use your power wisely because the computer will do exactly what you ask it to do.

The correct solution »

```
True
```

Add this to your current Elo rating »

Your Elo	Correct	Incorrect
0 - 500	47	-8
500 - 1000	47	-8
1000 - 1500	44	-11
1500 - 2000	22	-33
>2000	9	-46

Your current Elo rating »

1692

5.42   Quicksort

Puzzle 42

```
##############################
## id 195
## Puzzle Elo 1672
## Correctly solved 67 %
##############################

def qsort1(L):
    if L:
        return qsort1([x for x in L[1:] if x <
        ↪  L[0]]) + L[:1] \
                + qsort1([x for x in L[1:] if x
                ↪  >= L[0]])
    return []

def qsort2(L):
    if L:
        return L[:1] + qsort2([x for x in L[1:]
        ↪  if x < L[0]]) \
                + qsort2([x for x in L[1:] if x
                ↪  >= L[0]])
    return []

print(qsort1([0, 33, 22]))
print(qsort2([0, 33, 22]))
```

Puzzle 42: Which function correctly sorts the list?

This puzzle introduces a recursive algorithm to sort lists. When executing the functions, you get the following results.

```
print(qsort1([0,33,22])) -> output:   [0,
22, 33]
print(qsort2([0,33,22])) -> output:   [0,
33, 22]
```

So, based on this output, the function qsort1 correctly sorts the list. But why? The algorithm is a variant of the popular quicksort algorithm. Quicksort selects a pivot element from the list. In the puzzle, it selects the first element of the list, i.e., L[0]. Then, the algorithm moves all elements that are smaller than the pivot to the left side. Similarly, it moves elements that are larger or equal than the pivot to the right side.

This is repeated in a recursive manner for the left and the right lists. Suppose you create a new list as follows. You put all elements that are smaller than the pivot on the left, then the pivot, then all elements that are larger or equal the pivot on the right. The resulting list feels a bit more sorted, right? If the two sublists were already sorted, the list would be perfectly sorted. This is where the recursive call of qsort1 comes into play. It takes over the problem of sorting each sublist by applying the same scheme of pivoting and recursion to the sublist.

In contrast, the `qsort2` function appends both sublists to the right of the pivot element. Hence the list is already unsorted after the first recursion level.

Solving these kinds of puzzles regularly will boost your code understanding skills. They not only train your language understanding but also your conceptual thinking which is even more important for coders at any level.

The correct solution »

>   qsort1

Add this to your current Elo rating »

Your Elo	Correct	Incorrect
0 - 500	47	-8
500 - 1000	47	-8
1000 - 1500	44	-11
1500 - 2000	23	-32
>2000	9	-46

Your current Elo rating »

17 15

5.43 Unpacking Keyword Arguments with Dictionaries

Puzzle 43

```
#############################
## id 369
## Puzzle Elo 1673
## Correctly solved 30 %
#############################

def func(val1=3, val2=4, val3=6):
    return val1 + val2 + val3

values = {"val1":9, "val3":-1}
print(func(**values))
```

Puzzle 43: What is the output of this code?

Programming is about using lower-level functionality to create higher-level functionality. In general, any programming language is a collection of functions that in turn build upon functions provided by the operating system. You must master the art of building your own code with the help of existing functionality. Do not reinvent the wheel!

Functions are generic code snippets that can be tailored to your needs via keyword arguments. The puzzle shows a function that calculates the sum of three keyword arguments. The keyword arguments are initialized with a default value in case they are not defined by the function caller. The puzzle introduces two concepts: dictionaries and unpacking keyword arguments.

1) Dictionaries are Python data structures, defined via the bracket notation {}, that store key-value pairs. Python dictionaries work like real-world dictionaries: the keys are the words and the values are the explanations. You access the explanation to a given word via the index table. Similarly, in a Python dictionary, you access the values using the method of indexing. The indices (or keys) can be strings, integers, or any other immutable data type.

2) An interesting twist in the puzzle is to deliver keyword arguments via a dictionary using the **-operator. The **-operator unpacks the key-value pairs in the dictionary and matches those with the keyword arguments. As the second keyword argument val2 is not declared in the dictionary, it is initialized to its default value.

The correct solution »

12

Add this to your current Elo rating »

Your Elo	Correct	Incorrect
0 - 500	47	-8
500 - 1000	47	-8
1000 - 1500	44	-11
1500 - 2000	23	-32
>2000	9	-46

Your current Elo rating »

1738

5.44   Infinity

Puzzle 44

```
############################
id 356
## Puzzle Elo 1701
## Correctly solved 40 %
############################

print("Answer")
while True:
    pass
print("42")
```

Puzzle 44: What is the output of this code?

The question in this puzzle is whether the second print statement will ever be executed. The body of the while loop consists of the **pass** statement. This statement tells the interpreter to do nothing. Although the while loop does nothing, the interpreter is trapped forever because the while condition is **True**. Thus, our program wastes scarce CPU cycles until the user interrupts the execution. Hence, no execution path will execute the second print statement. It is interesting that 60% of finxters get this puzzle wrong.

The correct solution »

Answer

Add this to your current Elo rating »

Your Elo	Correct	Incorrect
0 - 500	47	-8
500 - 1000	47	-8
1000 - 1500	45	-10
1500 - 2000	25	-30
>2000	9	-46

Your current Elo rating »

1763

5.45 Graph Traversal

Puzzle 45

```
#############################
## id 274
## Puzzle Elo 1729
## Correctly solved 44 %
#############################

def has_path(graph, v_start, v_end, path_len=0):
    '''Graph has path from v_start to v_end'''

    # Traverse each vertex only once
    if path_len >= len(graph):
        return False

    # Direct path from v_start to v_end?
    if graph[v_start][v_end]:
        return True

    # Indirect path via neighbor v_nbor?
    for v_nbor, edge in
    ↪    enumerate(graph[v_start]):
        if edge: # between v_start and v_nbor
            if has_path(graph, v_nbor, v_end,
            ↪    path_len + 1):
                return True

    return False

# The graph represented as adjancy matrix
G = [[1, 1, 0, 0, 0],
     [0, 1, 0, 0, 0],
     [0, 0, 1, 0, 0],
     [0, 1, 1, 1, 0],
     [1, 0, 0, 1, 1]]
print(has_path(graph=G, v_start=3, v_end=0))
```

Puzzle 45: Is there a path between vertices 3 and 0?

A simple and effective way to grow your computer science skills is to master the basics. Knowing the basics sets apart the great coders from the merely intermediate ones. One such basic area in computer science is graph theory—which we address in this puzzle.

So first things first: what is a graph? You already know data structures like lists, sets, and dictionaries. These data structures are denoted as *complex data structures*—not because they're difficult to understand but because they build upon other data structures. A graph is just another complex data structure for relational data.

Relational data consists of *edges* and *vertices*. Each vertex stands in one or more relations with other vertices. An example for relational data is the Facebook social graph. Facebook represents users as vertices and friendship relations as edges. Two users are connected via an edge in the graph if they are (Facebook) friends.

How to maintain a graph data structure in the code? The puzzle uses an *adjacency matrix* as graph data structure G. Each row i in the matrix stores the out-neighbors of vertex i. And each column j stores the in-neighbors of vertex j. Thus, there is an edge from vertex i to vertex j, if G[i][j]==1.

How to determine whether there is a path between two vertices? The function find_path(graph, v_start, v_end, path_len) checks whether there is a direct or indirect path between two vertices v_start and v_end in graph. We know that there is a direct path between v_start and v_end if both are already neighbors, i.e., graph[v_start][v_end]==1.

However, even if there is not a direct path, there could be an indirect path between vertices v_start and v_end. To check this, the algorithm uses a recursive approach. Specifically, there is an indirect path if a vertex v_nbor exists such that there is a path v_start $\rightarrow$ v_nbor $\rightarrow$ ... $\rightarrow$ v_end.

The variable path_len stores the length of the current path. We increment it in each recursion level as the current path length increases by one. Note that all paths with length $\geq n$ consist of at least n vertices. In other words, at least one vertex is visited twice and a cycle exists in this recursion instance. Hence, we skip recursion for paths with length greater or equal than the number of vertices in the graph.

This puzzle asks whether there is a path between 3 and 0. If you understand what the code is doing, it suffices to look at the adjacency matrix G. There is a direct path from vertex 3 to vertices 1 and 2 (and to itself). But neither vertex 1 nor 2 has any out-neighbors. Therefore, there is no path from vertex 3 to any other vertex (besides vertices 1 and 2).

The correct solution »

    False

Add this to your current Elo rating »

Your Elo	Correct	Incorrect
0 - 500	47	-8
500 - 1000	47	-8
1000 - 1500	45	-10
1500 - 2000	26	-29
>2000	9	-46

Your current Elo rating »

1785

5.46 Lexicographical Sorting

Puzzle 46

```
#############################
## id 371
## Puzzle Elo 1748
## Correctly solved 44 %
#############################

pairs = [(1, 'one'),
         (2, 'two'),
         (3, 'three'),            · f o~
         (4, 'four')]

# lexicographical sorting (ascending)
pairs.sort(key=lambda pair: pair[1])
print(pairs[0][1])
```

Puzzle 46: What is the output of this code?

The high Elo indicates that only experienced Python coders can solve this puzzle. There are two barriers to overcome.

First, the lambda function seems to be an abstract concept. Yet, it is only old wine in a new bottle. A lambda function is nothing but an anonymous function with a special syntax. The variable name(s) between the lambda keyword and the colon (:) define the function arguments. The body after the colon uses the arguments to define the return value of the function. In the puzzle, we use the lambda function as a key for the sorting function. The key defines that the list should be sorted by the second value of the tuple, which is a string.

Second, we are not sorting by ascending integers, i.e., 1, 2, 3, 4, but by ascending strings according to their position in the alphabet, i.e., 'four', 'one', 'three', 'two'. So the second tuple element from the first list element is 'four'.

The correct solution »

    four

Add this to your current Elo rating »

Your Elo	Correct	Incorrect
0 - 500	47	-8
500 - 1000	47	-8
1000 - 1500	45	-10
1500 - 2000	27	-28
>2000	10	-45

Your current Elo rating »

5.47 Chaining of Set Operations

Puzzle 47

```
##############################
## id 399
## Puzzle Elo 1749
## Correctly solved 40 %
##############################

# popular instagram accounts
# (millions followers)
inst = {"@instagram":232,
        "@selenagomez":133,
        "@victoriassecret":59,
        "@cristiano":120,
        "@beyonce":111,
        "@nike":76}

# popular twitter accounts
# (millions followers)
twit = {"@cristiano":69,
        "@barackobama":100,
        "@ladygaga":77,
        "@selenagomez":56,
        "@realdonaldtrump":48}

inst_names = set(filter(lambda key:
↪  inst[key]>60, inst.keys()))
twit_names = set(filter(lambda key:
↪  twit[key]>60, twit.keys()))

superstars = inst_names.intersection(twit_names)
print(list(superstars)[0])
```

Puzzle 47: What is the output of this code?

You will use or have already used the concepts introduced in this puzzle. They are elementary pieces of knowledge for any Python programmer. There are three basic concepts in the puzzle.

First, we have the two dictionaries mapping an account name to the number of followers. For example, Cristiano Ronaldo (key: `"@cristiano"`) has 120 million Instagram followers. In contrast to lists, dictionaries allow fast data access. You can retrieve each item with only one operation without having to iterate over the whole data structure. In the words of a computer scientist: the dictionary access has *constant runtime complexity*.

Second, the filter function returns a new sequence in which each item matches a defined characteristic. The filter function takes two arguments. The first argument is a function that returns a boolean value `True` or `False`: `True` if a sequence element should be included and `False` otherwise. The second argument is the sequence to be filtered.

Third, intersecting sets `s1` and `s2` returns a new set that contains elements that are in both sets `s1` and `s2`.

The only star that has more than 60 million Instagram AND twitter followers is Cristiano Ronaldo.

The correct solution »

    @cristiano

Add this to your current Elo rating »

Your Elo	Correct	Incorrect
0 - 500	47	-8
500 - 1000	47	-8
1000 - 1500	45	-10
1500 - 2000	27	-28
>2000	10	-45

Your current Elo rating »

5.48 Basic Set Operations

Puzzle 48

```
############################
## id 390
## Puzzle Elo 1755
## Correctly solved 60 %
############################

words_list = ["bitcoin",
              "cryptocurrency",
              "wallet"]
crawled_text = '''
Research produced by the University of
Cambridge estimates that in 2017,
there are 2.9 to 5.8 million unique
users using a cryptocurrency wallet,
most of them using bitcoin.
'''

split_text = crawled_text.split()
res1 = True in map(lambda word: word in
↪   split_text, words_list)
res2 = any(word in words_list for word in
↪   split_text)
print(res1 == res2)          True
```

Puzzle 48: What is the output of this code?

After executing the code in the puzzle, both **res1** and

`res2` store whether the variable `crawled_text` contains a word from the `word_list`. I explain both ways to achieve this in the following.

`res1`: The map function checks for each element `word` in the `word_list` whether `word` is an element of the split `crawled_text`. The default split function divides the string along the whitespaces. The result is an iterable with three booleans, one for each word in the `word_list`. Finally, we check whether one of them is True.

`res2`: The any function checks whether there is an element in the iterable that is True. As soon as it finds such a True value, this function returns True. Note that it is more efficient to use the `any` function to do this instead of performing a list iteration. After checking for the first word 'bitcoin', the function already returns True.

The correct solution »

```
True
```

Add this to your current Elo rating »

Your Elo	Correct	Incorrect
0 - 500	47	-8
500 - 1000	47	-8
1000 - 1500	45	-10
1500 - 2000	28	-27
>2000	10	-45

Your current Elo rating »

1844 + 28 = 1872

5.49   Simple Unicode Encryption

Puzzle 49

```
############################
## id 391
## Puzzle Elo 1763
## Correctly solved 66 %
############################

def encrypt(text):
    encrypted = map(lambda c: chr(ord(c) + 2),
    ↪   text)
    return ''.join(encrypted)


def decrypt(text):
    decrypted = map(lambda c: chr(ord(c) - 2),
    ↪   text)
    return ''.join(decrypted)


s = "xtherussiansarecomingx"
print(decrypt(encrypt(encrypt(s))) ==
↪   encrypt(s))
```

Puzzle 49: What is the output of this code?

You already know that computers only operate on 0s and 1s. Every single character in a string is encoded as a sequence of 0s and 1s. Unicode is one such encoding that maps a bunch of zeros and ones (a binary ordinal value) to a symbol that you can read (a character). The Unicode table assigns one binary or decimal value to each character. For example, the Unicode value 41 encodes the value 'A' and the Unicode value 42 the value 'B'.

With Unicode, we create our own secret language via encryption and decryption functions. The functions **encrypt** and **decrypt** operate on a string literal **s1**. To encrypt or decrypt a string, we shift each character by two Unicode positions. The **encrypt** function shifts the string to the right, the **decrypt** function shifts it to the left.

We use the **map** function to implement this shift for each character in the string **s1**. Using the built-in function **ord()**, shifting a character is as simple as adding a bias value to the Unicode value of the respective character.

The result of both encryption and decryption is a sequence type. Hence, we join the sequence with the empty string as a separator to receive the final encrypted or decrypted string.

By calling the function **encrypt()** twice, the string is simply shifted by $2 + 2 = 4$ positions in the Unicode table. Hence, the result of a double encryption plus a single decryption is the same as a single decryption, i.e.,

$2 + 2 - 2 = 2.$

The correct solution »

True

Add this to your current Elo rating »

Your Elo	Correct	Incorrect
0 - 500	47	-8
500 - 1000	47	-8
1000 - 1500	46	-9
1500 - 2000	28	-27
>2000	10	-45

Your current Elo rating »

1972 - 28 - 1844

5.50 The Guess and Check Framework

Puzzle 50

```
#############################
## id 400
## Puzzle Elo 1780
## Correctly solved 56 %
#############################

import random


def guess(a, b):
    return random.randint(a, b)


def check(x, y):
    return y ** 2 == x


x = 100
left, right = 0, x
y = guess(left, right)
while not check(x, y):
    y = guess(left, right)
print(y)
```

Puzzle 50: What is the output of this code?

∧↺

The method of guess and check is a good starting point for designing a new algorithm. The algorithm is simple, parallelizable to thousands of cores, and well established in theory. The runtime of the algorithm can often be analyzed statistically.

The idea is to first guess (generate) a possible solution and then check whether it is correct (or acceptable). For example, Bitcoin miners guess the solution to a complex problem. If they find a solution, a new bitcoin is created. When generating the solution, it is common to use randomization. The efficiency of the algorithm depends on how informed the guessing is. The better you guess, the more efficient the algorithm becomes.

The puzzle finds an integer solution for the square root of an input number x. The guess method generates a random number y between 0 and x. It is not informed. The check method checks whether the number y is the square root.

The correct solution »

10

Add this to your current Elo rating »

Your Elo	Correct	Incorrect
0 - 500	47	-8
500 - 1000	47	-8
1000 - 1500	46	-9
1500 - 2000	29	-26
>2000	10	-45

Your current Elo rating »

1844 25-1873

— 6 —

Final Remarks

Congratulations, you made it through 50 code puzzles and you have significantly improved your skills in reading and understanding code. By now, you should have a fair estimate of your skill level in comparison to others— be sure to check out Table 3.1 again to get the respective rank for your Elo rating. This book is all about pushing you from beginner to intermediate coding level. In follow-up books, we address the advanced level with more difficult puzzles.

Consistent effort and persistence is the key to success. If you feel that solving code puzzles has advanced your skills, make it a daily habit to solve a Python puzzle and watch the related video that is given on the Finxter web app. This habit alone will push your coding skills through the roof—and provide a comfortable living for you and your family in a highly profitable profession. Build this habit into your life—e.g., use your morning coffee break routine—and you will soon become one of the best programmers in your environment.

Where to go from here? I am publishing a fresh code puzzle every couple of days on our website `finxter.com`. All puzzles are available for free. My goal with Finxter is to make learning to code more efficient, more individualized to your precise skill level, and more accessible— that's why I also post regular puzzles on our Facebook page. For any feedback, question, or problem you struggle and need help with, please send me an email to `info@ finxter.com`. If you want to grow your Python skills on autopilot, register for our free puzzle newsletter at `app.finxter.com/accounts/register/`.

Finally, I would like to express my deep gratitude that you have spent your time solving code puzzles and reading this book. Above everything else, I value your time. The ultimate goal of any good textbook should be to *save, not take,* your time. By working through this textbook, you have gained insights about your coding skill level and I hope that you have experienced a positive return on invested time and money. Now, please keep investing in yourself and stay active within the Finxter community.

35245126R00115

Printed in Poland
by Amazon Fulfillment
Poland Sp. z o.o., Wrocław